THE CRISIS IN COMPARATIVE
LITERATURE

THE CRISIS
IN COMPARATIVE
LITERATURE

by

RENÉ ETIEMBLE

Translated, and with a Foreword, by
HERBERT WEISINGER and GEORGES JOYAUX

MICHIGAN STATE UNIVERSITY PRESS
EAST LANSING
1966

Contents

Foreword

Comparative literature is at once a subject of study, a general approach to literature, a series of specific methods of literary history, a return to a medieval way of thought, a methodological credo for the day, an administrative annoyance, a new wrinkle in university organization, a recherché academic pursuit, a recognition that even the humanities have a role to play in the affairs of the world, close-held by a cabal, invitingly open to all; but first and foremost, it is an attitude of mind. Not surprisingly, comparative literature finds itself very much in the same position academically as does the United Nations diplomatically. Essentially, it consists of an unstable amalgam of competing literary nationalisms not a few of whose citizens react to mention of it in ways not too dissimilar from those of certain nationals of the countries contained within the United Nations to mention of UNESCO. Yet just as the nations of the world have banded together out of equal fear and hope of the future in the shaky cause of political internationalism, so literary history and criticism have turned to comparative literature to absorb the shock of intellectual internationalism which twentieth-century technology, communication, political events, and social change have thrust as much on literature and literary study as on the circumstances from which they derive. This is not to say that literature and literary history have only now discovered cosmopolitanism—from at least the Renaissance on, the trade between literatures has been keen and lucrative—but only that as the pace of technological, economic, political, and social interdependence has so rapidly accelerated within the past few decades, so has the pace of cultural interdependence quickened. Comparative literature is thus a scholarly response to a decisive shift in point of view with regard both to the way in which literature is studied and to the ways men must live in an increasingly intertwined world; the winds of change blow as strongly across the plains and rivers and established campuses of Europe and the United States as they do across the jungles and mountains and burgeoning campuses of Africa and Asia.

Only because it is an attitude of mind can comparative literature withstand being squeezed into the restrictive molds into which many of its zealous practitioners seek to cast it. For there is no agreement as to what it is, except that it is a good thing, and of course even this harmless proposition is hotly denied by the chauvinists of the traditional departments of literature. Its tutelary gods, then, are Procrustes, the divinity of narrow definition, and Proteus, the ruler of amorphous shapes, and since they are but fraternal twins, their brotherhood extends only to their scientific nomenclature. Like Eteocles and Polynices, they have led their followers into fierce fratricidal war to determine sole hegemony over the kingdom of comparative literature. Only the epic pen of the Homer who composed the Batrachomyomachia could do justice to the bitter struggle: the crushing cost of typing paper, the reckless expenditure of books and articles, the cries of anger shattering the customary calm of academic halls where international conferences are held, the heedless slaughter of many brave professors whose epitaphs, self-written, lie chastely graved in the pages of Comparative Literature, Yearbook of Comparative and General Literature, Revue de littérature comparée, and other professional journals.

> Dulce et decorum est
> Pro patria mori.

Yet, like the unhappy sons of Oedipus, they have succeeded only in killing themselves off, not, however, in dramatic single combat, but out of sheer boredom and pointlessness. For whatever it is or ought to be, comparative literature continues to be taught and practiced, and in ever increasing volume. For the sake of the record, it ought to be pointed out that comparative literature has been taught and practiced from at least the time Cicero rendered his decision on the Asianist-Atticist problem and Horace used Greek examples to arrive at his definition of tragedy.

René Etiemble's book must therefore be seen as the rainbow of academic peace raised after the storm of scholarly controversy. For until its appearance France was the unbreachable redoubt of comparatism, narrowly conceived as a limited number of specific methods for the study of a limited number of specific relations between literatures, from which, on orders of Baldensperger, Carré, Guyard, Hazard, Munteano, Roddier, and Van Tieghem, persistent attacks were launched against the enemy overseas, the much more loosely conceived programme of American comparatism which, secure in its numbers and budgets, responded in kind, Brown, Levin, Peyre, Remak, and Wellek commanding. But with the appearance of Etiemble's little manifesto, the battle may now be declared over, though an occasional sniper's shot in a rearguard action may still be heard. French and American comparatists, as well as those of other lands, ought now to be able to agree that comparative literature is a series of methods of literary study held together by a common attitude of mind. It seeks to establish the relations between literatures in as many different ways by as many different methods as can be devised; it limits neither the choice of subject nor the means by which it can be examined, and, indeed, it endeavors constantly to add to its store of objects of inquiry as well as to its arsenal of investigative techniques. The battle is over, yet one cannot help noting the irony that this battle of the books should have been fought by nationalist partisans over how internationalism in the study of literature should be attained; as always, what nationalism inspires in creative drive it destroys in xenophobic rage.

The consequences of this shift in point of view are therefore worth considering. It is obvious that no man can now master even

his own chosen province of study, let alone the entire map of
knowledge made available to him by the proliferation both of fields
of investigation and of the results of research in them; a glance at
the annual Shakespeare bibliography alone will dash whatever
hopes might be entertained along those lines, no matter how firmly
one buckles down to the task. The expert is thus forced to know
more and more about less and less; the non-specialist, once outside
his own ever-contracting area of competence, is, with all the good
will in the world, forced to know less and less about more and
more. In other words, the very acceleration and increase in the
quantity of information have become intrinsically self-negating;
the more that pours into the common pool of knowledge does not
thereby mean that any one individual drinking of it is therefore
any the wiser for the abundance. The Baconian dream of social
utility via the royal road of accumulation has collapsed, and with
it the corollary notion that knowledge can be made divisible into
a multiplicity of smaller and smaller, and therefore more manage-
able, parts. The mere addition of the parts does not result in the
recreation of the whole of which they are the constituents; the
whole is different from its parts and possesses a life and a meaning
quite other than the life and meaning of its components, a difference which is not one of quantity alone but of quality and which
therefore calls into play different methods of observation, assimila-
tion, and judgment. Put another way, one leaps from description
to evaluation with a corresponding elevation of criteria. Oddly
enough, the preoccupation with separate parts tends to end up
with the denial of the individuality of those parts through the use
of statistical methods in which the individual disappears in the
average behavior of gross phenomena, whereas concern for the
quality of the whole concentrates on the perception of the nuances
of differences in individual behavior; macroscopic agglomerates
appear as though destined to a dull and dreary fate, but the ultimate particles of which they are constituted seem rather to lead
cheerfully independent existences. That this awareness of the interdependence of knowledge has begun to make its weight felt on the
advancement of learning is signified by the attempts in many and

diverse fields of inquiry to see things in living relation to each other, as, for example, field theory in physics (not to mention the unified theory or the eight-fold way), ecology in biology, systems methods in engineering, gestalt in psychology, phenomenology in traditional philosophy, historicism in history, and the rise of inter-disciplinary fields such as bio-physics. Thus the atomistic approach to the pursuit of knowledge is giving way to, or more precisely, is making room for, another mode of inquiry in which the analysis of things as such is being supplemented by the synthesis of the behavior of things vis à vis each other. Comparative literature is the application of this mode of inquiry to the study of literature.

Comparative literature, then, springs from two sources, the inter-dependence of peoples and the interdependence of knowledge, and these in turn arise from the transformation of the conditions of contemporary life stamped on them by the irresistible impact of the technology of the twentieth century. We can no more avoid viewing literature and its study in the perspective of international interdependence than we can pretend that wars in Asia, the grow-ing pains of nascent nationalism in Africa, overpopulation in India, and poverty in Latin America cannot affect us. We accept quite readily the ability of the other arts to cut across the lines of time and space yet balk when it is suggested that literature is no less able to transcend the same limitations on the chauvinistic grounds that it is above all the national character of a particular literature which gives it its distinction and which is therefore alone the proper focus of our attention. Putting aside the perhaps dubious evidence of the talkative Englishmen, the blond Italians, the dark-haired Swedes, the phlegmatic French, and the scrutable Orientals regularly met with on one's travels, no foreigner could (if such were indeed the case) ever possibly penetrate the mystery of an-other literature, and we are therefore wasting our money, time, and effort on trying to teach Americans French, German, Italian, Greek, or what have you, not to mention our political and elee-mosynary commitments abroad, and so on for each country in relation to all the others; we should simply have to opt out of the life of our own times. Yet we see no occasion for surprise that the

Merce Cunningham Dance Company should be invited to go on tour by the Sarabhai family in Ahmedabad; that it should be well received in Prague and enthusiastically applauded in London; that its designer, Robert Rauschenberg, should win the Grand Prize in the Venice Biennale; and that its musical director, John Cage, should be seriously attended to by European composers. That they are all Americans might provoke a flutter of mild patriotism; that they describe themselves as "representatives of the far-out, experimental, avant-garde" is faintly amusing; but that they dance, paint, and compose in ways meaningfully communicable to diverse peoples and having essentially nothing to do with national character tells us something significant about the communicability of the arts, and the same observation can be made of the serious cinema of France, Italy, Sweden, and Japan. But traditional literary history tends to look on such transactions with a suspicious eye, even though writers themselves have never hesitated to engage in the international trade of styles, ideas, and motifs; and where they have gone, we have no other choice but to follow them. So typically an English poet as Shakespeare drew his sources from English translations of French translations of Italian versions of stories drawn from the international storehouse of tale; so typically an American poet as Frost had to make his reputation in England; and even so typically an insular poet as Wordsworth learned a thing or two in France.

In a wry sense, then, comparative literature is a revival of the intellectual ambitions and mode of thought of medieval Latinity as it has been so lovingly described by Curtius, though in far different circumstances, for far different reasons, and with far different results. The goal of medieval Latinity—a universal culture expressed in a universal language and comprehended in a universal mode of thought—was a dream destroyed by religious and secular power struggles, the inflexible limitations of a stratified social structure, and fatal commitment to an untenable system of belief. Comparative literature has no such grandiose aims; it proposes only that the literatures of the world be understood in relation to each other; yet even this modest aim has been subject to the pressures of nationalism and bloc politics. Etiemble himself, who on one page speaks so glowingly of the virtues of internationalism, cannot on another refrain from taking snide cracks at the United States (after all, what forces a Frenchman to drink Coca-Cola, except perhaps the taste of the Algerian red which is foisted off on him as table-wine); the comparatists from the other side of the Iron Curtain sometimes sound as though comparative literature were a weapon of the West in the cold war (the picture of the CIA plotting comparative literature studies would be entertaining were it not that it reveals a frame of mind frightening in its self-imposed blindness); and even so humane a scholar as Curtius can embrace a vision no larger than Europe. Indeed, many comparatists, having managed to emancipate themselves from the thrall of nationalism, promptly enslave themselves in the larger, but still confining, concept of the primacy of the Western literary tradition. They insist that without mastery of Greek, Latin, German, French, and English the study of comparative literature cannot be pursued. That the Western literary tradition is the mother of our minds and the nurse of our sentiments cannot be doubted; that all comparatists must know it as specialists is, however, quite another proposition. If comparative literature is to be free to grow, it cannot be made exclusive, and it must provide the student who is interested in the inter-relations of the Eastern literatures on each other (a subject no less complex and certainly as demanding as the inter-relations of the Western literatures on each other) with the tools he needs, with the same care it shows toward the student who is occupied with the influence of Poe on the French symbolists. If we expect of the student of Eastern literary relations Chinese, Japanese, Urdu, Tamil, and Bengali, and Greek and Latin and German and French and English, why not expect of the student of Western literary relations Greek, Latin, German, French, and English and Chinese and Japanese and Urdu and Tamil and Bengali; one is as absurd as the other. The Western world now stands at the pinnacle of power, but it was not always so, nor is it necessarily likely to remain so; and we, as scholars who stand—or who ought to stand—for a way of life not measurable in mundane terms, have a special obligation to hold up the standard of international tolerance. In the first article in the first number of The Yearbook of Comparative and General Literature, Peyre wrote: "The most crying need of our time . . . is for more imagination, so that we may conceive, sympathize with, and strengthen ways of life different from our own." These words were written over ten years ago; they are even more pertinent today.

It is at this point that Etiemble's plea for the value and dignity of translations is most persuasive. Let us face the fact honestly: there are not many of us who have the gift of languages, and even those enviable masters of several languages must pale at the almost weekly announcements of a new language and literature in process of emerging or a forgotten one newly recovered. But we need not go that far; an example closer to our own Western tradition makes the recognition of the respectability of translation immediately obvious. Most of us, at one time or another, have concerned ourselves with the origin and development of tragedy and of the theory of tragedy; many have learned Greek to be able to read the Athenian playwrights and Aristotle's Poetics in their own words; some have even taught themselves Arabic in order to disentangle Aristotle from his medieval commentators; and a few have acquired Hebrew to separate the medieval Arabic commentators from their medieval Hebrew influences. But if we are fully to understand the idea of tragedy, we have to trace its roots to the myth and ritual of the ancient Near East. Are we then to learn to read the Sumerian and Egyptian and Akkadian and Hittite and Ugaritic texts in the original languages before we can dare say a word on this subject, not to overlook the necessity of comparing and contrasting the myths of the ancient Near East with the myths of India, Iran, China, Japan, Mexico, Oceania, Africa, and of the Amerindians before they can be understood? We are particularly fortunate in the high quality of the translations now being produced by a devoted group of scholar-poets who are redoing Greek and Latin classics in language sensitively responsive to the modern ear, yet even more faithful to the text than earlier versions; translations of the ritual texts of the ancient Near East are now based on the most genres, ideas, themes, and attitudes is surely of no less importance, and for such studies translations, provided that they are reliably done (Frenz has carefully documented the problems here), must be used after a certain point is reached, the most obvious delimiting factor being, as Etiemble sensibly points out, the average life-span of a man. After all, the ability to read a language does not automatically carry with it concomitant taste and judgment, and these, at bottom, constitute the ends of literary study; we know that Browning's Grammarian settled hoti's business, but we do not know what he thought of it. After decades of squirming away from the social origins and effects of literature, we are once more face to face with the critical problems raised by literature as institution and as revelation, or, if this is thought too pretentiously put, simply literature as communication. This is not to say that comparative literature has standards of evaluation built into it; the sources of one's judgment lie deeper and are more complex and derive from areas of experience of which literature is but one portion; but the insistence on inclusiveness which comparative literature compels exerts in turn pressure in the direction of literary judgment.

Another brake on comparative literature is the timidity with regard to expanding the scope of its objects of inquiry, particularly so far as the relations of literature to the other arts are concerned. Indeed, it can be argued that as a general rule the art historians have made better use of literature than the literary historians have made of art. Yet one's own experience with the art of one's own time testifies that the arts do not exist apart from each other; a morning visit to the Guggenheim, an afternoon concert sponsored by the Group for Contemporary Music at Columbia University, and an evening in an off-Broadway theatre are evidence enough that the arts enjoy a lively and mutually inspiring symbiosis. Subject to the same pummelling of experience, motivated by the same forces, reacting to them in similar ways, and pushing toward the same conclusions (non-conclusions perhaps would be more accurate today), their responses are indeed necessarily different with respect to the differences in the media employed, but are far less apart with respect to the symbols, motifs, ideas, and techniques

meticulous scholarship; Ibsen, Strindberg, and the major Russi
can be read in translations marked both by accuracy and sense
style; Latin American classics are being opened up to us; and it
an encouraging sign of the times when a writer of Nabokov's rep
tation can put out a translation of and commentary on Pushkin
critical acclaim (by and large).

The truth is that comparatists, like their colleagues in the d
partments of national literatures, are still frightened by the ghost
raised by the New Critics. That different literatures are written in
different languages is a truism; that each language possesses qualities which differentiate it from others and give it its unique character, its genius so to speak, is no less true; that writers in the same
language reveal differences in style derived from their individual
manipulations of the language is likewise true. But equally not in
dispute is the fact that language is not only sui generis but is as
much, and in the same way, a carrier of communication; language
both is and says. The doctrine of the aesthetic self-containedness of
the work of literature must be in the long run self-defeating; a
tautology cannot by definition advance beyond itself. Speaking of
the post-war generation of critics, Hassan has recently said that
"they are anxious to assert themselves against the rigors and pieties
they have inherited," that they "are loath to consider the literary
work merely as an object," and are equally "reluctant to believe
that contemplation is the sole reaction to it"; "the critic now
wishes," he declares, "to entertain the possibility that action may
be a legitimate response to art." Put more brusquely, this simply
means that the new generation is tired of criticism as mere para-
phrase and restatement (often longer and certainly less poetic than
the poem under dissection, not to mention the intrusion of values
where none or others have been proclaimed) and wants to take up
again in open and direct fashion questions of value and judgment.
For those who are concerned with stylistics, mastery of the language or languages involved is of course beyond question, but comparative stylistics, though relatively neglected and in need of
encouragement, is but one branch of many of comparative literature. The study of transmission and transformation of forms,

which they use, and there is no reason to assume that it was otherwise in the past, as the art historians have been successfully demon-
strating. As a matter of fact, changes in style and in attitude are
more sharply revealed in art than in literature, since motifs can be
more clearly defined and since variation in them can be so graphi-
cally illustrated; one sympathizes with the note of envy of the
critic of the plastic arts which Levin has sounded in The Gates of
Horn. This technique has long been the strength of the Warburg
school in which the history of art, literature, and ideas has been
expertly and exquisitely mixed. "Just as it is impossible for an art
historian to interpret his material without a knowledge of what was
thought, written and practised in the environment in which the
work was produced," Panofsky has declared, "so it is impossible for
a literary historian to understand all the implications of a piece of
poetry or prose unless he knew with what kind of pictures or images or with what kind of descriptions or discussions of pictures the
writer had been familiar." And he gives this illustration:

> When Shakespeare in Timon of Athens makes fortune beckon to
> her favorites with her "ivory hand" one would not do justice
> to the simile if one were to interpret it merely as a flattering
> comparison of Fortune's skin with ivory; one has to know that
> old representations showed Fortune bipartite, so to speak, with
> one-half of her face and one of her hands painted dark in order
> to stress the idea of Fortuna Adversa, the other half of the face
> and the other hand light in order to emphasize Fortuna Secunda.
> This is only one very small instance of the infinitude of analogous
> cases in which the prose writers and poets of the past had a defi-
> nite image in mind while shaping their metaphors and similes.

The instance may be small, but it is precise, accurate, and illuminating.

Once the full force of the methodological thrust of comparative
literature has been assimilated, it becomes necessary to readjust the
perspective in which literature has been hitherto depicted. If, up
to now, we have pictured literature as a series of parallel columns
separated by vertical national lines, we must now redraw the graph:
the vertical lines need to be erased and we must show instead how

the same phenomena appear in country after country, though at different given times; the dividing lines, if such devices are to be useful at all, must be horizontal. This does not mean that we are unaware of the dangers inherent in form, period, and style concepts. But we are no less aware of the equal danger of persisting in what Wellek has termed "external factualism and atomism," lest literature and the study of literature both are quite drowned in a flood of data without meaning. Wellek has well defended the continued usefulness of even so slippery a concept as baroque in this way: "Whatever the defects of the term baroque—and I have not been sparing in analyzing them—it is a term which prepares for synthesis, draws our mind away from the mere accumulation of observations and facts, and paves the way for a future history of literature as a fine art." No one is under the illusion that the fact that Donne and Herrick lived but a few years and worked but a few miles apart from each other and wrote in the same medium turns them both into mannerist poets, nor that because the arts employ certain terms in common—spatial, temporal, coloristic, rhythmic, linear, and the like—that these words must mean precisely the same in every case, else they cannot be used. But because such relationships cannot easily be found does not mean that they cannot ultimately be found, or that the search for them must be abandoned forthwith; it is incredible that men of such sensitivity and sophistication as Eliot, Mann, O'Neill, Van Der Rohe, Picasso, and Stravinsky could have lived in the same world—a world so violent in its provocations—at the same time, without responding in ways which can be subsumed within like categories, differences in national origin and media notwithstanding. If this injunction had been heeded, we should now be without the exciting and exacting scholarship of—we omit instances drawn from comparative literature itself for obvious reasons—Cassirer's The Philosophy of Symbolic Forms, Eliade's Patterns of Comparative Religion, Ferguson's Music as Metaphor, Giedion's The Eternal Present, Hyman's The Tangled Bank, Kahler's The Tower and the Abyss, Lovejoy's Primitivism and the Idea of Progress, Niebuhr's The Nature and Destiny of Man, Nygren's Agape and Eros, Panofsky's

Gothic Art and Scholasticism, Toynbee's A Study of History, and Thompson's Growth and Form, to mention no others.

If the final justification of learning is the use which may be made of it, then the end of literary scholarship is preparation for criticism. Comparative literature serves criticism by functioning both as a telescope and as a microscope. Used as a telescope, it widens the range of relevance and enlarges the frame of reference in which the individual work is placed; it winnows out the accidental, the local, and the parochial; and it thus provides the basis for critical norms founded on the fullest possible range of examples. Used as a microscope, it narrows and sharpens the frame of reference and thus differentiates the individual, unique qualities of particular works of literature from others in their own genre, form, style, and period. On the one hand, a telescopic view of the sources Shakespeare used for his plays demonstrates the extent of his reliance on tradition and his acceptance of conventional themes, methods of presentation, and ideas. On the other hand, a microscopic examination can show Shakespeare's own hand at work. To discover what he did with his sources, to follow his manipulations of them, to see what he took over, left out, augmented, diminished, recast, and added to on his own is to be on the track of the uniquely Shakespearean, those very qualities which single him out from among all the others who used the same stuff of creation but who could not see in it and make of it what he did. Scholarship unbalanced by criticism tips over into pedantry; criticism unstabilized by scholarship veers over into irresponsibility; together they serve as the gyroscopes which curb each other's excesses. This is not to argue that comparative literature is in itself the act of criticism, only that it brings that act closer to realization.

We are not unaware that a note of truculence has insinuated itself into our discussion as though we defy anyone to deny that comparative literature exists; yet, if pushed to the wall, we should meekly lay down our arms and readily admit that, in a certain sense, there is no such thing as comparative literature as such. That certain sense is of course quixotic, but, in all seriousness, it is our hope that the attitudes and techniques of comparative literature

will permeate and suffuse in and through the traditional departments of national literatures so that, instead of being drawn from
and then drawn off from the traditional departments, the comparatist approach will be exemplified, not merely in comparative
literature programs alone, but everywhere where literature is studied and taught. For, as we have insisted again and again, art recognizes no boundaries and needs no passports; the march of ideas,
themes, motifs, forms, and attitudes cannot be halted by the
linguistic, political, and cultural barricades which have been thrown
up by the accidents of time and place. No matter what his special
field of study may be, then, the conscientious student of literature
must cross the borderlines of nation, language, and discipline in his
efforts to understand as much as he can of what goes on in the work
with which he is concerned. If he wishes to uncover the origins
of Herbert's imagery, he will cross over into iconography as did
Tuve; if he wants to paint in the background of the battle of the
books, he will pioneer the study of the rise of scientific ideas as did
Jones; if he wants to explicate The Fable of the Bees, he will un-
ravel the intricacies of eighteenth-century economic thought as did
Kaye; if he wants to track down the sources of The Ancient Mari-
ner, he will ransack the books of travels which Coleridge devoured
as did Lowes. It does not matter whether he calls himself a comparatist or not; it matters only that he should be willing to do
justice to the work itself, no matter where it leads him.

   This does not mean that the comparatist can see no merit in the
Balkanization of culture; on the contrary, to insist only on the similarities and uniformities of peoples, cultures, and literatures is to
shut one's eyes to the wonderful variety of men and their ways and
correspondingly to the no less wonderful variety of the literatures
they have produced. The comparatist refuses to be laced into the
strait jacket of an either/or position; for him, it is not a question
of dedicating one's allegiance to determining the distinctive qualities of a national literature to the exclusion of a like dedication to
discovering only what literatures have in common: the proper study
of literature recognizes as much the variety in uniformity as it does
the uniformity in variety. In the long run, however, literature is

limited by the ultimate limitations in the nature of man himself; it cannot transcend the scope of his mind, his imagination, and his emotions; it can concern itself only with the problems with which he himself is concerned, which he himself sees, sets, and seeks to solve. Thus, though an almost proliferation of subjects and their possible treatments may well be granted, it must in the end be reducible to those subjects and their treatments which men have thought worth treating to begin with, and these turn out to be fewer in number than we might at first expect. The ultimate core of human nature—whatever we might define it to be—seems finally to be occupied by the same questions—of life and death and the future life, whether here on earth or elsewhere; of birth and growing up; of the challenges to the emerging person; of marriage and family; of love and ambition and joy, and of overcoming the obstacles in their path; of hate and anger and fear and sorrow, and of their consequences; of despair and of hope; and all that tragic protest against the utter indifference of a universe too large, too strange, and too unconcerned for human comfort, comprehension, and control; and around these few great central themes literature wondrously weaves its manifold threads, over and over again, into new and unforeseen shapes, countless in their variety, yet single in their origins and purpose. Art does not shape, it reshapes; the artist does not create, he recreates; the reader does not experience, he re-experiences. Making, considered in all its aspects, is thus a profoundly social phenomenon: it is men calling to each other across the gulfs of separation in which they are enisled, and it is the role of comparative literature to sharpen our ears to this call.

Just as the hot, strong hues of individual difference may blind the eye from the total perception of the picture of which they are the parts, so the uniform gray of similarity may blot out the unique virtues of separate parts, and this is true no less of art than of life. We cannot emphasize difference at the expense of similarity any more than we can concentrate on similarity at the cost of difference. Hence the value of Etiemble's insistence on our being aware of the existence of ways of thought and behavior alien to our own, and in their own terms; our world is now too closely linked and too interdependent for us to dare neglect any part of it, if only for the selfish reason of our own survival. But there is a better reason, the appeal of common humanity; as we learn more and more about the different ways of men, we learn as much about the universal in man. To voyage with Odysseus, to cry aloud with Oedipus, to rage with Lear, to laugh with Don Quixote, to love with Don Juan, to defy with Ahab, to despair with K is to voyage, cry aloud, rage, laugh, love, defy, and despair with particular men of particular times and particular places, but we can do so only as we can transcend the difficulties of those particulars, even at the moment of savoring them, and participate in their common humanity. This is the justification of those disciplines we call the humanities, of which comparative literature is most profoundly one.

We have suggested that comparative literature springs from two sources, the interdependence of peoples and the interdependence of literature itself. By this we mean not only the inter-relations between literatures as they are commonly understood but the very integrity of literature itself, as an art and as a voice. Modern scholarship and criticism have so anatomized literature into its parts and parts of parts that it stands in danger of losing its essence as art. No one has been more greatly indebted to the insights into literature which have been derived from fields outside it—psychology, anthropology, the history of religion, philosophy, sociology, and the like—than we ourselves have, and, like Wellek, we freely acknowledge that debt. We go even further: we would lay it down as a general rule that the study of literature grows only as it receives infusions from outside itself, from the application of ideas and methods first developed in other fields and then fitted to the study of literature which, when it is left to itself, slows to a halt and ends by eating itself. But, like Wellek, we are equally concerned that in the enthusiasm for cross-fertilization from these new ideas and methods the recognition of the unique character of literature as an art, as a distinct mode for apprehending, comprehending, and organizing experience, a way no less valuable—we would contend even more valuable, but this is not the place for polemic—than others, but different from them, will be forgotten. Comparative literature is a constant reminder that literature is the vessel in which the spirit of man, of all men, is stored. We are not arguing for protecting the epistemological virginity of either literature or criticism, as the followers of Cassirer and even Wellek himself appear to do; we are convinced that neither literature nor criticism can nor ought to escape from the life out of which they come and in which they must live; we wish only to affirm that literature and the study of literature have a high and distinct place in that life and that to allow them to curl up into the contracting circle of coterie causerie, as a child does when he is afraid, because our technological society seems indifferent and even hostile to them is to lose the battle for the human spirit before it has even begun. The determination to wage this battle and hopefully to win it is firmly implanted in comparative literature. Nowhere has this intention been given more forceful expression than in a stirring passage by Wellek which, we believe, must surely gain the assent of all comparatists:

> But once we conceive of literature not as an argument in the warfare of cultural prestige, or as a commodity of foreign trade or even as an indicator of national psychology we shall obtain the only true objectivity obtainable to man. It will not be a neutral scientism, an indifferent relativism and historicism but a confrontation with the objects in their essence: a dispassionate but intense contemplation which will lead to analysis and finally to judgments of value. Once we grasp the nature of art and poetry, its victory over human mortality and destiny, its creation of a new world of the imagination, national vanities will disappear. Man, universal man, man everywhere and at any time, in all his variety, emerges and literary scholarship ceases to be an antiquarian pastime, a calculus of national credits and debts and even a mapping of networks of relationships. Literary scholarship becomes an act of imagination, like art itself, and thus a preserver and creator of the highest values of mankind.

A man who has made his reputation in fields far different from, and, we must candidly confess, more demanding and more, much more, fraught with good or ill for all mankind than comparative literature, recently said: "There is a quality in art which speaks across the gulf dividing man from man, nation from nation and century from century." Coming from a non-specialist, that is not at all a bad definition of comparative literature; as an injunction, as a guide to what we ought to be doing, it cannot be bettered.

THE CRISIS IN COMPARATIVE
LITERATURE

I

INTRODUCTION

A Crisis in Comparative Literature?

Krise des Komparatistik, Crise de la littérature comparée, The Crisis of Comparative Literature—probably this is being repeated even in Serbian, Japanese, and so on. Granted that the word "crisis" is fashionable today, and granted that to solicit the reader's attention the authors of articles or books on any and all subjects flaunt the word everywhere, like the red light of a brothel, comparative literature has indeed been suffering, for at least the past two decades, from what may well be called a crisis. I intend here to make a diagnosis of this crisis with the purpose of prescribing, or at least suggesting, a few remedies.

Against all chauvinism

Marius-François Guyard, Professor of Comparative Literature in the Faculty of Letters of the University of Strasbourg, published in 1951, in the series *Que sais-je?,* the first edition of a work primarily directed to the general reading public, but in fact much discussed by specialists, *La littérature comparée.* Even though he fortified himself with a preface written by Jean-Marie Carré, Professor at the Sorbonne, the book was coolly received in various places, especially in the United States. In a review attacking this work, Calvin S. Brown maliciously noted that our countryman classifies comparative studies under the following headings: "French Writers outside France," "Foreign Writers in France," "Influences among Foreign Literatures." Who would, under these circumstances, dare forbid American comparatists the right to give their own literature "the same central position"? But then, who would deny the Arab, or at least the Moslem, the right to avail

3

himself of the fact, undeniable at least to him, that his is God's tongue, and to demand that a literature so endowed with this unique privilege should dominate all others? Even more, on the strength of a population which will soon reach the billion mark, buttressed moreover by a recognized civilization going back 4,000 years, and on the strength of its very name, the "Central Empire," why should not China claim for its literature the same privilege which Guyard as a good patriot claims for his? As a citizen of the United States, a country perhaps too willing to parade its power, Calvin S. Brown is therefore not unjustified in challenging Guyard's premise. Such procedure is indeed pointless; "in that way madness lies."

When I applied for the Chair of Comparative Literature at the Sorbonne, made available by the death of Jean-Marie Carré, I did not at all hide the fact that, were I to be accepted into this Institution, I would try to introduce a different conception of our discipline. When I was elected, Rector Sarrailh of the University of Paris opened the pages of the *Annales de l'Université de Paris* to me to expound my point of view. Limited as I was to article length, I wrote a few pages entitled "Littérature comparée, ou, comparaison n'est pas raison."[1] Shortly before, a special issue of the *Revue de littérature comparée* (January-March, 1953) devoted to "Orientations en littérature comparée" seemed also to answer, in its own way, Guyard's theses; besides the French conception, it also gave the German, American, and Italian points of view. Franco Simone referred to Croce's aesthetics and recalled that Luigi Foscolo Benedetto rightfully considered that "literary criticism and literary history are two distinct disciplines, both equally legitimate." But if the American contributor thought our discipline to be "somewhat centrifugal," a German contributor virtually equated Western literature with universal literature. Yet what a pity that no study brought us news of comparative literature in Russia. It is true that Stalin's tyranny had forbidden the study of this bourgeois science in Russia. Thus in 1950, writing in *Pravda*, did not Fadeiev, dicta-

---

[1] "Littérature comparée ou comparaison n'est pas raison," *Hygiène des lettres*, Volume III (Paris: Gallimard, 1958), 154-173.

tor of the writers, condemn Georg Lukacs, finding him guilty of comparatism, that is to say, of cosmopolitanism, of having a bourgeois mind (in fact, almost of complicity with the capitalists)? Fortunately, however, times have changed. Since 1958 the *Societas scientarium Lodziensis* of Łódź University in Poland has been publishing, under the direction of Stefania Skwarczyńska, Jan Trzynadlowski, and Witold Ostrowski, a review, now in its eleventh volume, whose title in three languages is in itself a program: *Zaganienia Rodzajów Literackich, Voprosy Literaturnyn žanrov, Les problèmes des genres littéraires*. In 1962 (26-29 October), the Hungarian Academy of Sciences organized in Budapest an International Congress of Comparative Literature in which not only the representatives of the socialist world—with the exception of Albania and China—participated, but representatives as well from Belgium, Switzerland, Holland, and France, including, *ex officio*, W.-A.-P. Smit, President of the International Association of Comparative Literature. Now that, freed from Stalin's presence, the socialist world recognizes that our discipline answers the fundamental requirements of Marxism, comparative literature, conceived in Guyard's terms, appears even more provincial. At the very time when *Voprosy Istorii*, 1958, reproaches Soviet scholars for isolating themselves from the rest of the world (since one cannot understand Lomonossov without referring to European culture, nor the Russian revolutionary democrats without knowledge of the thought of the utopian socialists of France and England), is it not ironic that a new edition of Guyard's *Littérature comparée* should appear in which he does not change a jot of what he wrote in 1951?

Against all provincialism

This attitude is all the more strange since the whole world, or not far from it, is now involved in comparative studies. Witness, the Centro de investigationes de literatura comparada de la Universidad de Chile, or the works published in Peru by Estuardo Nuñez, *Autores germanos en el Perú* (Lima, 1953) and *Autores ingleses y norteamericanos en el Perú* (Estudies de literatura comparada, Lima, 1956), or, in keeping with the strictest rules of the French school, Raúl Porras Barrenechea's *Los Viajeros italianos en el Perú* (Lima, Ecos, 1957); and, a more moving witness still, considering the political circumstances, Jakob Ben Iechouroun's work on *Le Lyrisme russe et son influence sur la poésie hébraïque* (I am giving in French the title of a work published in Hebrew in Tel Aviv, Dvir Editions, 1955): it appears that not only the themes and images but also the turns of phrase of contemporary Jewish poetry bear the imprint of Russian classics! I need not point out to the Japanese the existence of the *Hikaku Bungaku, Journal of Comparative Literature*, published by the Comparative Literature Society of Japan, or the *Hikaku Bungaku Kenkyu, Études de littérature comparée*, published by the Institute of Comparative Literature of the University of Tokyo.

Politics and Comparative Literature

The first of the tasks required of comparatists is to renounce, from now on, every variety of chauvinism and provincialism, to recognize at last that the civilization of mankind, in which values have been exchanged for thousands of years, cannot be understood or appreciated without constant reference to those exchanges, whose complexity demands that we do not center our discipline on but one single language or one single country.

This is not tantamount to forbidding this or that country, or this or that group of peoples, from interesting themselves in questions which concern them more intimately. Yet, even in this case, politics must not be permitted to interfere and thus falsify the prosecution of such studies. Consider the address with which Mrs. I.-G. Nieoupakoïeva, following Vianu, opened the Congress in Budapest, in 1962. After praising the French school and criticizing the American school which seemed to her seriously to denationalize literatures, this influential member of the Moscow Academy of Sciences condemned the tendency of the capitalist world to study the comparative history of European literatures in isolation. Yet, at the same time, she approved one of the themes of the Budapest

Congress: namely, initiating the comparative study of literatures of
Eastern Europe and the Balkans. In substance I replied to her:
If you admit, and I for one am willing to do so, that for geographical, historical, and political (in today's terms) reasons the
socialist world is more particularly justified in studying the cultural and especially literary relations of the Danubian countries in
the east and southeast of Europe, then you will have to admit that
for the same geographical, historical, and political reasons, the
peoples of Western Europe are equally justified in studying more
particularly the cultural and especially literary relations between
the countries which were civilized by Rome, that is to say, Italy,
the Iberian peninsula, France, England, Western Germany, and
even North Africa. Let us make sure that, in the East as well as in
the West, these regional comparative studies are not used for political manoeuvering.

In the concept which certain Germans have of comparative literature, I sometimes hear the echoes of the European dream which
Hitler revived, very much as so many others did before him, and
which rightly worries our Soviet colleagues no less than it does us.
Surely Europe did not have to wait for this mad man to feel and to
want to be united; surely Rome, Charlemagne, Charles V, Louis
XIV, Napoleon, and Bismarck prove to us that, behind differences
in languages, a single Europe has endlessly struggled to emerge—
at times succeeding, as in the period from the Classical World
to the Middle Ages, from the Renaissance to the Enlightenment,
and from the First Empire down to our own times. However, comparative literature should not, in the wake of the tentative outlines
of a reconstituted Europe of which the Common Market and Eu-
ratom are so far the most spectacular examples, attempt to create,
for the benefit of a conservative and catholic Europe, a new center
of the world, at once dogmatic and dangerous. Neither should the
socialist countries, now drawn together by a common ideology, use
this ideology as a pretext to neglect or vilify their traditional and
immediate relations with Western Europe. Luckily, all kinds of
communications and reports presented at the Budapest Congress
by delegates from the socialist countries suggested that Mrs. Nie-

oupakoïeva's views stressed a theoretical position (with which I had already been acquainted through a number of Soviet publications), which other delegates mitigated with discrimination and sometimes even forcefully. The closing speech and the provisions of the final resolution proved that, in spite of some differences in the use of vocabulary—differences which will perhaps be further diminished some day (I have in mind especially the use of such words as *realism, critical realism, socialist realism*, which have quite different meanings according to the political background—socialist or capitalist—but to which Louis Aragon's recent speech, *Discours de Prague*, could restore a common meaning)—comparatists from the capitalist world and those from the socialist world are in agreement on the essentials: the object and the methods of their common discipline.

One might well hope, therefore, that an article such as *National-literaturen und Europäische Literatur*, written by Professor Horst Rudiger of Mainz and published in the May, 1962 issue of the *Schweitzer Monatshefte*, does not mean a return to a European chauvinism which, though less narrow, would not be much better than the French chauvinism of Marius-François Guyard.[2] It is, perhaps, not completely without reason that, despite its merits, Ernst Robert Curtius' essay, *Europäische Literatur und lateinisches Mittelalter* gives rise to worry among the comparatists of the socialist countries. On the other hand, when Mrs. Nieoupakoïeva attacks René Wellek's report during the Second International Congress of Comparative Literature (held in Chapel Hill, 1958); when she disputes the temperate and so often judicious article of Henry H. H. Remak, "Comparative Literature at the Crossroads: Diagnosis, Therapy and Prognosis"; when she reproaches Henri Peyre for asserting that the most estimable trait of comparatism is undoubtedly the supranational consciousness which it succeeds in imparting to men, I am forced to discern in this a clear manifestation of her Russian patriotism, a patriotism which must not de-

---

[2] A chauvinism which, as Professor Mortier of the University of Brussels pointed out, is an improvement on that of a Louis Raynaud who condemned Romanticism because of its German origin.

generate into a new distrust of the cosmopolitan mind (not in the bourgeois meaning of the word, but in its Socratic, in its Montanist meaning).

Comparative Literature is Humanism

Thus, it seemed to me useful to recall, at the Budapest Congress, two formulae, which I see as the credo of all comparatists:

> The previous local and national isolation in which each one was self-sufficient is being replaced by a universal interdependence of nations. What is true of material production is equally applicable to intellectual production. A nation's works become the common property of all nations. National narrowness of mind and xenophobia are becoming more and more impossible; from the roots of numerous national and even provincial literatures henceforth will flower a universal literature. (Karl Marx)

> If I knew something useful to me but injurious to my family, I would reject it from my mind. If I knew something useful to my family but not to my country, I would try to expunge it. If I knew something useful to my country but prejudicial to Europe, or else useful to Europe but inimical to mankind, I would view it as a crime. (Montesquieu)

What a scandalous paradox if today capitalist countries alone were becoming capable and desirous of affirming in comparative literature the internationalist principles of Montesquieu and Karl Marx!

These points established, I was pleased to hear our colleague from the Moscow Academy of Sciences maintain that comparative literature must study not only relations between different literatures in the modern and contemporary period, but also, in its totality, the history of these relations, even if it meant going back to the most ancient past. Mrs. Nieoupakoïeva, who shows so much sympathy for the French school of comparative literature, reminds me, quite *à propos*, that the teaching of our discipline at the Sorbonne is in the hands of an *Institut de littératures modernes comparées,* and that, traditionally, studies there are pretty much limited to the international relations starting only at the 16th and 17th centuries, with special emphasis on the 19th and 20th. It is as though the study of relations between Greek and Latin literatures could not, or was not, supposed to interest us! It is as though the relations between the Greek world, the Arab world, the Hebrew world, the Latin world, the Slavic world, and the Mongol Empire in the Middle Ages were not worthy of our attention. It is as though when dealing with the origins of tragedy and comedy, the comparatist could, nowadays, ignore Canon Etienne Drioton's book, *le Théâtre égyptien*, an indispensable prelude to any consideration of Greek tragedy and comedy, and consequently of European drama.

As for Japanese comparatists, if after the Meiji era they have been quite rightly interested in the relations of their country with American and European literatures, if they have good reasons to study the influence of English poetics on Japanese prosody, the influence of English and Italian letters on Natsume Soseki; or of French literature on Akutagawa Ryanosuke, how could they, without betraying the spirit of our discipline, neglect the ancient and lasting relations which united them to China and the Buddhist world? When Koichi Sakai examines the influence of the *Tch'a king* on the *Chashin Monogatari*, he engages in the same activity as the Frenchman who examines how the myth of Theseus, the myth of Oedipus, and the myth of Prometheus have been utilized by Cocteau and Gide.

Will it be objected that, already prodigiously stretched in space —since it pretends to cover the whole planet—our study of comparative literature will become so in time as well, and that consequently no teacher will be able to obtain more than its rudiments, were he to labor all his life? I answer that I am limiting myself so far to defining the *spirit* of our discipline. Our concern at the moment, however, is to examine whether one can reconcile the requirements of our profession with the average length of the life of a man—even a comparatist.

II

CRUCIAL QUESTIONS:
Bibliographies
and working languages

The Teaching of Comparative Literature Must be Centralized

These being the conditions which comparative literature must meet, it is proper therefore to indicate how this goal is to be reached.

Decentralization is in style, and so much the better, since any excessive centralization means bureaucracy, tyranny, excessive development of certain universities at the expense of some, and the downgrading of still others (I have especially in mind what happens in France where Paris has devoured everything). Although decentralization has its virtues, and important ones, there will be no comparative literature worthy of the name until research and teaching in this discipline is centralized. What can be said of these universities—unfortunately many—where a single professor, by himself, at times, though not always, helped by an assistant, is supposed to undertake the teaching and direct the research? In fact, what can be said of Institutes where two or three professors, provided with four or five assistants, must, in principle, be responsible for all the courses, direct all the papers, and supervise all the dissertations? This system is equally "mad." The result is well known: in the countries I have in mind, only half a dozen overworked subjects are ever taught, about which, moreover, the professors assign only two or three texts which will be plagiarized without any increase of knowledge in the field. What can be said of countries, France in particular, where comparative literature professors must popularize, because of competitive examinations whose programs change every year, subject-matter which thus can be and must be nothing but superficial? In my opinion, comparative literature will be seriously taught only when each of the countries interested in it will organize at least one Institute, grouping 15 to 20 professors, a corresponding number of assistants and research directors, selected not only for their broad education, but in such a way that all the large families of languages be sufficiently represented, relative to their role. Even if it specializes in modern comparative literature, what is the value of an Institute in which only Germanic and Romance languages are studied with but an occasional excursion into the Slavic world? The Institute I dream of would naturally include Hellenists and Latinists, but also Sumerian scholars and Egyptologists, Slavicists, Hindi and Bengali specialists, sinologists, Germanic and Romance language scholars, Semiticists, men familiar with Finno-Ugrian, Turko-Mongol, and Dravidian literatures, and I do not forget Japanese! Everything is interdependent in the history of literatures, and he who does not have more than a little insight into a rather large number of literatures will never understand—and I mean understand—a single literature. To limit myself to the country I am best acquainted with, France, at the present, could support only one such Research Institute, since it is in Paris and in Paris only that one can learn, besides the Romance, Slavic, and Germanic languages, all those other languages which I believe are indispensable.

As for libraries and reading rooms, such an Institute should have at its disposal considerable funds. Now, how much would be saved by suppressing those ridiculous provincial libraries, crowded with books scattered everywhere, and which I could easily do without. Every essential is lacking in these libraries and therefore each by itself is worthless. Even if one were to allocate to a single center, in a single Institute, the funds thus wasted because they are now so dispersed, one would still be far from being able to equip it with periodicals, rare works, and microfilms. Governments, which waste money right and left, should agree to finance our discipline.

For a bibliography

For lack of a serious bibliography, how can these libraries be created? Besides the fact that it is extremely difficult to consult, the *Bibliography of Comparative Literature*, prepared by Fernand Baldensperger and W. P. Friederich, is quite inadequate. Even if one lined up end to end the bibliographies of the *Yearbook of Comparative and General Literature*, of the *Revue de littérature comparée* (now abandoned), of the *Regesten* (critical reports published every three months in Dutch, by the Institute of Comparative Literature of the University of Utrecht), of the Japanese periodicals, one would still be unable to keep up with what is being published. If one admits, as I do, and as the Russian comparatists now do, that we must also become interested in the relations between Asia (Near and Far) and Europe, between Europe and Latin America, etc. . . ., these bibliographies will appear still more useless. Certainly, we must thank the Pen Club of Japan for having provided us with a precious bibliography of European translations of Japanese works, in *Japanese Literature in European Languages*; certainly, we should thank the American Council of Learned Societies for having collected, under the direction of Martha Davidson, *A List of Published Translations from Chinese into English, French and German*; certainly, the Moscow Library of Foreign Languages has provided us with a bibliography of Russian translations and critical studies of Chinese literature published in Russian. Learned Societies in Poland also have given us a catalog of Oriental publications, and the Belgian Commission for bibliography a work by Jaqueline Senny, *French Translations of Oriental Literatures*; these we acknowledge. I do not forget either the *Index Translationum* published by UNESCO since 1948. Dealing only with translations, these are only the first elements of bibliographies which, to be useful, should include and examine systematically all the significant books and articles in the field of comparative literature. What is the use of a bibliography which is not analytical? I would prefer it to be critical, but what is the use of hoping? Among the thousands of books and articles from all over the world which I examined and classified, and continue to read and classify for the bibliography of *Le Mythe de Rimbaud*, how many would deserve to be listed in a serious study, not of comparative sociology, nor of the comparative history of literatures, but of comparative literature? Ten to twenty at most! Those are the studies toward which the work of bibliographers should guide us. I do not conceal from myself the realization that this wish appears ridiculous in the present state of the world. I will therefore be satisfied, in a modest way, with a fairly analytical bibliography. If we cannot have this as the minimum, we should shut the doors of our Institutes. This bibliography should be completed by a central index of all comparative literature studies in progress everywhere. For lack of this, one will see several scholars wasting years on the same subject. I will cite just one example: an Egyptian proposed to me several years ago a subject whose importance I had discovered while teaching at the University of Alexandria: the influence of the French theater on the birth of an Arab-language theater in Egypt, from the 19th century on. She had been collecting materials for a year, when another Egyptian came to see me in my office; without telling anyone, he had for years been studying the influence of our dramaturgy on the renaissance of the Egyptian theater. Patiently, he had acquired, classified, and examined many translations and adaptations of French plays, farces, and comic operas, performed in the most modest theaters of his country. Naturally, from now on, he alone would treat the subject. Now, let us suppose that instead of coming to me, the Egyptian girl, married to a diplomat stationed in London, had proposed her subject to some British university: two compatriots who did not know each other would thus have treated the same subject, though only one of them was qualified, since he had sole possession of a large amount of materials which exist only in single copies.

How can this bibliography and this index of research be obtained? Very simply! It would be sufficient if organizations such as our *Centre National de la Recherche Scientifique* understood that just as it is of importance to the strength of nations to maintain excellent bibliographies dealing with mathematics, physics, and chemistry, so the reputation, and perhaps even the very survival of nations, would in no small way be affected by the financing of bibliographies useful to the humanist, and notably bibliographies of comparative literature. Let us suppose that the National Commission of each member state of UNESCO sponsored an analytical bibliography of comparative literature studies published in its country. Let us suppose that it assembled an index of all the works in progress in the country. UNESCO could then centralize, and continually keep up to date those bibliographies and indices. We would then have at our disposal materials with which to prepare the equivalent of the bibliographies already at the disposal of the specialists in the sciences.

While waiting for this wish to be granted to us, let us hope that the socialist world will contribute to the grand work by preparing the bibliography whose establishment was desired at the Budapest Congress. Even if the Academies of Science of the socialist countries were to limit themselves to assembling a bibliography dealing with comparative literature in the communist countries what a boon that would be to us!

The Working Tools

A question arises immediately, that of the languages for our work. The comparatist of the generation of Baldensperger and Paul Hazard could limit himself to two or three languages, possibly four or five at most: German, English, Spanish, French, Italian. For us, that is no longer enough! As the Japanese have become more and more interested in comparative literature, European scholars see reviews with promising titles reach their desks, but only the abstracts are available to them. We will thus have to learn Japanese, or have all the numbers of *Hikaku Bungaku* and *Hikaku Bungaku Kenkyu* translated. Furthermore, in the last issue I received of the *Jadavpur Journal of Comparative Literature*, a periodical published by the Institute of Comparative Literature of the University of Jadavpur, in Calcutta, I read, or rather I cannot read, besides several articles in English, a study in Bengali by Manabendra Bandyopadhyay. Europeans and Japanese will thus have to study this language, Bengali, before starting on Hindi, Urdu, Tamil, should Indian universities in one, the other, or the third of these languages become, in their turn, interested in comparative literature. There is reason to hope or to fear (it amounts to the same thing) that, faithful to the spirit of their former Andalusian civilization, the Arab world will revive tomorrow a discipline which would find in its Moslem past a huge domain, if not to pioneer—for Lévi-Provençal and several others have already worked at it—at least to exploit.

Not to forget Marathi, which I did a while ago, even though I am directing a dissertation treating of Molière's influence on Marathi literature via the influence of British literature. "Direct," what a curious way to speak!

It is true that I am also "directing" another dissertation which promises to be truly significant, *The Influence of French Poetics since Baudelaire on Hungarian Poetry of the 20th Century*. Neither should Finno-Ugrian languages be kept in the ghetto of our universe; after all, they gave us the *Kalevala* and Petöfi. Thus, if I want to study the *Kalevala*, I will be forced to study, besides Finnish, at least Russian, since one of the fundamental works on this epic has just been published by V. Jirmounski, *Narodnyi geroiceskij epos*, that is to say, *The Popular Heroic Epic*, a work which, according to the preface, has as its subject the examination of this genre in the Romance, Germanic, Russian and Southern Slavic languages, without forgetting the peoples of Central Asia and Karelia (the Karelo-Finnish Soviet Socialist Republic). Yes, everything in our discipline is interdependent, and no one can, henceforth, concern himself seriously with any question whatsoever without reading works in at least a dozen different languages.

When one is French, moreover, how can one pretend to be involved in comparative literature while neglecting the question of the bilingualism of Malagasy, Arab, and Vietnamese writers, the similarities between the *hain-tenys* of the Merinas and Eluard's poetry, the influence of French poetry on contemporary Vietnamese poetry, the influence of colonial literatures or of colonies on the motherland and its literature, etc. The situation can only grow worse, since, being almost completely freed from colonialism, Black Africa will probably want to restore certain languages, which will claim the title of languages of civilization (Peul, Bantu, and how many others?). For lack of knowing them, no one will be able to appreciate the role of the Negro substratum in African poems of the last one hundred years written in French or in English. Since the socialist world is now going to contribute to the enrichment of our discipline, how many more languages will become indispensable to the comparatist! In order to read the excellent review published by the University of Łódź *Zagadnienia Rodzajów Literackich*, one must know, besides Polish, German, English, French, Italian, and Russian. In addition to the *Acta Litteraria Academiae Scientiarum hungaricae*, which deal, in languages generally accessible to the comparatist, with such questions as "Heine, die Weltliteratur und die ungarische Dichtung," or "Petöfi et la littérature tchèque," there now appear in Budapest reviews written entirely in Hungarian, *Filológiái Közlöny* (*Philological Bulletin*) and *Helikon Világirodalmi Figyelö*, (*The World Observer*) in which one finds, in Hungarian, studies and reports which we would be wrong to ignore. Who knows how soon Serbian, Czech, Rumanian, not to mention "Brazilian," will become indispensable tools for the European comparatist? On the other hand, it is difficult to imagine a Japanese comparatist interested in his distant past who would ignore Chinese, Sanskrit, Pali, and Tibetan; and it would likewise be regrettable if he deprived himself of the works dealing with these questions written by Western-language Buddhist scholars, which is the equivalent to saying that he too, to excel in his discipline (that is, our discipline), will be responsible for ten to twelve languages.

Not every one is as fortunate as the Central Europeans who, located at a confluence of races, nations, languages, and religions, and endowed with idioms which, despite all their virtues, have not gained a currency equal to that of their German, English, Russian, French, or Italian counterparts, must therefore learn, besides their own, four or five languages, which they do indeed acquire and generally know quite well. The English and French in particular, because they benefitted from tongues which were for various reasons almost universal throughout yesterday's world, are generally less well equipped in foreign languages than their colleagues from Central Europe and the Slavic world. What was striking at the Budapest Congress was that the three working languages, German,

French, and Russian, were understood by almost all the partic-
ipants, with the exception of those from Western countries, the
best equipped being able at most to read Russian. To be sure, our
Slavic specialists in comparative literature were not in attendance,
but on the whole, this Congress strengthened my belief: in the
20th century, the comparatist can no longer ignore either Russian
or Japanese. And what will happen tomorrow if China should
reconsider its stand and decide to pursue our discipline!

How many years will it take, then, to prepare the comparatist
who will be capable of practicing and teaching his discipline around
1990 or 2000? The passive knowledge of a foreign language requires
at least one year of sustained effort; an active knowledge, much
longer. If we limit ourselves to requiring from the comparatist a
passive knowledge of foreign languages, ten to twelve years of preliminary training will be needed. Twenty to twenty-five years devoted to foreign language study will be necessary if an active knowledge of the working tools is required of him. So that our discipline
is soon going to stumble against the obstacle which threatens to
impede the progress of human knowledge: Babelism. How can that
be remedied? How is it possible to train professors who will not
feel out of place in the world in which they will live, a world in
which the students they will teach will, in turn, teach others who
will live in 2050 and still later? From time to time, a man appears
in the field of comparative literature whom the chances of history
have magnificently equipped: René Wellek, for example, who, of
Czech origin, raised in Central Europe, and an emigrant to Anglo-
Saxon countries, is equally at home in Slavic, Germanic, and Romance languages. Edouard Gaède is another example: born in
Poland, equally skilled in Russian, English, German, and Polish,
favoured with a better than average knowledge of Latin and Greek,
and capable of writing in French a work of rare quality, *Nietzsche
et Valéry*.[3] If one must rely on tyrannies and revolutions, and on
émigrés alone to recruit comparatists, it will be a long time indeed
before we have competent masters in sufficient number. Ah! if

[3] Paris: Gallimard, 1962.

only at the cradle, or shortly after, we could select gifted children, we could have them master, between the ages of two and fifteen, several foreign languages as remote from one another as possible: a utopia good at best for Plato's *Republic*. Let us find another solution!

Each of the countries where comparative literature is taught has its own traditions. In Germany, a discipline such as the *"romanistique"* gives students a good preparation for comparatism: besides several Romance languages, they know some Latin and Greek. In command of their own Germanic language, which opens to them, without too much effort, Dutch, Danish, Swedish, Norwegian, not to mention English, expected today of everyone, German Romanticists would excel in comparative literature studies dealing with Western Europe. Yet, curiously enough, they are not very much involved in such studies. The training of the French comparatist is quite different: sometimes they are *Agrégés* in Letters or Grammar, trained in French, Latin, and Greek, but who by chance or personal vocation have been led to modern foreign languages, generally two or three; or else, they are *Agrégés* in Modern Foreign Languages, very well at ease with two foreign languages, besides having some Latin and occasionally some Greek. The latter can also claim to study our discipline so long as they limit themselves to the Roman geographical area (but one must hope that they will never have to make use of a Russian book dealing with the subject). As it is practiced in Japan, the teaching of comparative literature requires of the student and professor knowledge of the important Western languages, and since he finds himself naturally in a Japanese, Buddhist, and Chinese milieu, he will be well equipped to study cultural relations between Asia and Europe, an ability which is unfortunately quite rare in European countries. So rare indeed, that those persons who are involved in these questions in France, Virgile Pinot (who studied the Chinese influence on our Enlightenment), Mrs. Iraldo-Goncet (who is presently studying the role played by the discovery of Japan in the formation of liberal ideas in the same period), have undertaken, and, in the case of Pinot, completed, their work without knowing a word of either Chinese or Japanese. This situation should not continue. To deal with first things first, I systematically apply the following idea: I demand that a student who wishes to work with me towards a State Doctorate either know or learn, in addition to the languages which each of us must know at least passively, to exercise his profession and to do a minimum of research, one or two of the languages less commonly studied in France. Several of them have started Chinese, others Japanese, still others Turkish, while some are learning Slavic tongues. I intend to guide one or two of them towards the study of Finno-Ugrian languages in order to prepare a team of comparatists who, in ten to twelve years, will be able to establish an Institute worthy of what our science (or our art) will become; an Institute where one could study the influence of Slavic metrics on Rumanian poetry; the relations (if there are any) between the Tibetan epic and that of the Finno-Ugrian peoples; the cultural relations between Mongols, Turks, and Russians in the Middle Ages; the influence of Japanese poetry on the so-called *haïku* written in German, Spanish and French; its influence on our *dodoitsu* and on our *tanka*.

Translators and Translations

Conceived in such a way, comparative literature should grant the art of translation its due. Using the pretext that, pressed for money, too many self-styled translators abuse at random, in a language they know rather poorly, a language they hardly know, university circles have bestowed a deplorable reputation on all translators, even the best. Now, if we remember the quality of the literary works produced in French by Valery Larbaud when he translated Samuel Butler, in Hungarian by the poet Tóth Árpád when he translated *Aucassin et Nicolette*, of Babits' *Divine Comedy*,[4] or Gyergyai's *Marcel Proust*, when one reads Saint John Perse's *Anabase* in T. S. Eliot's translation, how can one fail to admire the harmony between knowledge and art, between precision and delicacy in their work.

---

[4] See György Rába, "La Divina Commedia nella traduzione ungherese di M. Babits," *Filólogiai Közlöny Supplementum* (1961).

Some comparatists, particularly of the French school, feel that our studies should deal only with those languages which we at least read, if not speak. For some subjects, this theory is applicable: I cannot easily imagine a study of J. Kochanowski's influence on the poetry of the metropolitan Dositheus if one knows neither Polish nor old Rumanian.[5] But why force the researcher who wants to study the movement of ideas in general or the technique of the novel to limit his examination only to those novels and ideas whose texts he can read? To the extent that my dual capacity of professor and novelist forces me to be interested in the theory of the literary genre I practice, I know all the benefits I drew from reading *Gengi Monogatari* in Waley's English version, or the *Shilappadikaram* translated from Tamil into French, or further the Vietnamese novel *Kim Van Kiêu* in the version recently produced by Nguyen-Tran-Huan. If he has not read the *Hizakurige*, even in an English translation, or the *Si Yeou Ki* (*Hsi Yu Chi*), even in a French version, or Tolstoi and Dostoievski, even in German, what European will dare to speak of the novel in general? Not having admired, even in a French translation, Akinari Ueda's *Ugetsu Monogatari*;[6] not having known, even in translation, some of the *Séances* of Hariri; or several Jewish short stories published in the Middle Ages, who will dare to discuss the aesthetics of the short story? In fact, so far as I know, with respect to the Jewish short story, we have had, until recently, only Klausner's book, published in Hebrew in Tel-Aviv in 1947. Thus, must we learn Hebrew? I will be told that since then, Yehuda Arye Klausner published in an English version of his own a summary of his thesis in *Zagadnienia Rodzajów Literackich*, and that in 1952 a Spanish professor published in Barcelona a study more accessible to us, because of the language, and based entirely on Klausner's research. It is a fact! Still, how many other studies, published in Hebrew or in Japanese, in Polish or in Czech, in Hungarian or in Arabic, on subjects as worthy of our interest as this one, will forever remain dead to us,

---

[5] See L. Gáldi, "Un grand disciple roumain de J. Kochanowski: le métropolite Dosithée," *Studia Slavica* VI (1960), fasc., 1-2.

[6] *Contes de pluie et de lune*, translated by R. Sieffert (Paris: Gallimard, 1956).

hidden in periodicals little known by those nations which have at their disposal a more powerful or illustrious language.

Did not *Le Monde* inform us recently that two Tibetan monks have just been sent to Denmark by the Dalai Lama in order to translate a huge mass of documents gathered by Prince Peter of Greece: treatises on theology which are important to anyone interested in Buddhist thought? Will they be translated into Danish? If they are, all the Buddhist scholars will have to begin studying that language, or have those documents translated from the Danish.

Whether it is a matter of original works or critical studies dealing with our discipline, the role of translations—and therefore of translators—will increase decade after decade. In this area again, UNESCO, so often maligned, has understood its mission, and finances, here and there throughout the world, collections of *representative works* which, given the provincialism in which the mind which prides itself on its culture still lingers, and given the expenses involved in translating from rare or difficult languages, would not be profitable otherwise. Arabic and Iranian classics are now translated into Western languages, while European classics are rendered into Arabic and Iranian. Thanks to UNESCO, certain works of little commercial value from Latin America are published in France, and Gallimard's series "Connaissance de l'Orient," intends to make available to the Western public the best texts of Japan, China, India, and the Far East. To accomplish this objective, we lack competent translators. Comparative literature should thus concern itself with the training of excellent translators. Why do specialists of the French school, who could write a hundred pages on the role of the translator as "intermediary," decline to support the views of UNESCO and to train at the Sorbonne, besides conscientious archivists and assiduous researchers of notarized minutes, a team of men who, able to write well in their own language and trained in the scholarly rules of the *explication de textes*, would translate for us the richest, most beautiful works of the lesser known literatures? When Jean Paulhan revealed to the French in 1913, *hain-tenys* of the Merinas, it was the writer, at least as much as the Malagasy scholar, who served comparative literature. After more than a half century, his translation still stands, and the Malagasy praise it as a successful achievement, as much for the quality of the language as for the understanding of the genre. Gide was right in thinking that every writer should devote part of his life to enriching his literature with translations of some of the masterpieces he is capable of feeling, from among those written in languages he knows. Rare indeed are the French writers who have complied with this wish. Since translating will not give a man his bread and butter, only a few rich persons, with some exceptions, have enjoyed devoting themselves to this kind of activity: Gide, translator of Conrad and *Hamlet*; Proust, devoted to Ruskin; Valery Larbaud, already mentioned; Supervielle, translator of *As You Like It*, *A Midsummer Night's Dream*, and reviser of Juan Zorilla de San Martin's *Tabaré*. Let us train, therefore, and as quickly as possible, translators capable of handling, without distorting them, Hungarian, Bengali, Finnish, Tamil, Chinese, Tibetan, Malagasy. This means that teachers devoted to research will have to admit that translation, especially when it deals with difficult, almost inaccessible texts, requiring five, even ten years of work (which is the case for any great Chinese novel, or for the *Gengi Monogatari*), should be considered, not as an occupation for ladies or dilettantes, but with respect and as one of the essential tasks of our discipline. Provided that he pretends to be engaged in "research," any imbecile with an index file will be able to obtain a fellowship, funds, an Institute of his own, and will have no difficulty in publishing junk, scraps of garbage, whereas translators, in whom comparative literature is interested only as "intermediaries," seem to him quite unfit to live. Once more, UNESCO was right in wishing that Institutes of Foreign Languages or of Comparative Literature, in universities worthy of the name, should prepare translators of such quality that they would be assured of an adequate status and salary—which, in my opinion, should at least equal that of the "researchers," for a skillful translator is rare, much rarer indeed than the conscientious "researcher." In order to translate well, one must, above all, be a good writer in the language into which the material is to be translated.

But, in practice, we are looking for researchers, and are discouraging translators, though they are far more needed today.

For a few years, fortunately, the International Federation of Translators has been publishing, in collaboration with UNESCO (to which our discipline is very heavily indebted indeed), *Babel: International Review of Translation*, directed by Pierre-François Caillé. This review should help to give translators the place they ought to have in the 20th century. I do not refer only to the salary they deserve, and which, apparently, only socialist countries have given them. Recently, I met in Hungary a poet about forty years old who cannot yet, for good reasons, live on his poetry, but who is able, however, to manage quite well, thanks to the poems he has been translating for years. Here is the rate: five forints a line for an edition of 3,000 copies, seven forints for an edition of 5,000 copies, ten forints for 10,000 copies; thereafter, so that the translator does not become too rich, the rate diminishes. Assuming that a forint, which corresponds theoretically to twenty centimes (four cents), is worth 40 to 50 centimes (eight to ten cents) in terms of the standard of living, 100 lines, published in an edition of 10,000 copies would net him 800 to 1,000 forints, that is to say, the equivalent of 400 to 500 Francs ($80 to $100). The average salary of a clerk being about 1,000 forints a month in Hungary, one must admit that, taking into account the difficulty that a poem presents for the translator, and reducing the salary to 500 forints ($20) for 100 lines when 3,000 copies only are printed, the salary of the Hungarian translator can be considered fair. And if I think about the Japanese, I would remind them that in March, 1958, *Babel* devoted its whole issue to the difficulty presented by translation from Asiatic languages. A study by Mikio Hiramatsu, of Tokyo, "The Present Status of Japanese Translators," taught me that in Japan "there are only two or three professional translators who can make a living from their translations alone. These well-known translators must translate and publish ten works a year in order to provide for their needs and those of their families." You must admit that the situation is serious! In the capitalist countries only UNESCO, I believe, offers translators payment comparable to those of the socialist countries (and these are still not directly in proportion to the actual number of copies printed).

Once the questions of salary and status are settled, the recruitment and training of translators will be facilitated. Indispensable as they are in making the works themselves available to us, translators will never be numerous enough, as things go, to translate for us all the works dealing with our discipline in all the languages from all the countries interested in comparative literature. Will we then have to trust in machines to provide the information we require? Even then, we would be at a disadvantage when compared with mathematicians, physicists, and chemists. Besides the fact that the latter will obtain from their governments more translating machines than they will need, the very nature of automatic translation is better suited to the exact sciences than to those disciplines where the quality of the language counts, no matter how little. Even supposing, if we should obtain them, that these machines could provide us with translations of critical studies, which contain only raw information, needless to say such machines could never replace the translator when it comes to the sonnet, the *terza rima*, or the *haïku*, even free verse or prose.

A Universal Working Language?

If any discipline is in need of an international working language, it is ours! But which language? Esperanto, highly esteemed a little everywhere? To study literature, that is language shaped to a beautiful form, should we revert to an idiom which, though useful to scientists, could not possibly be beautiful? Should English, the language of communication of the capitalist world, be considered? Anyone who thinks that the socialist countries would accept the tongue of their rival, and at times slanderer, would be naïve. Russian? The same thing applies! French, which for two centuries, was for the white man the ultimate sign of culture? Although it has many friends, and though, for example, at the recent Budapest Congress, it found itself more often honored, despite the geographical and political situation, than Russian and German, the other official languages at the Congress, French counts among its Anglo-Saxon allies too many enemies to believe it possible that the course of history could be reversed and to presume that French could ever become, by virtue of its past merits, the future language of mankind. Latin, then, which unified Christian Europe, the Europe of the Renaissance, and further illuminated the Europe of the Enlightenment? Besides the fact that it is a dead language, except in Church (and even there! since at the Vatican Council now in progress, more than one Catholic prelate has envied the Protestant and Orthodox observers who have been provided with translators), it would be futile to imagine that the socialist world would accept as a universal language in comparative literature, or in the sciences, the language of its very enemy, the Catholic Church! This being so, what else can be suggested? For want of a universal working tool which, in the present state of the world, seems impossible to achieve, I choose another solution: the Chinese ideographs which would give us, if not a common language, at least a common writing form, a form which every one could read and pronounce in his own idiom, thus allowing each and every one of us to write his research in a language not too difficult of access to everyone else, and so be able to devote himself more thoroughly to the apprenticeship in the few languages required for our specialty. Unfortunately, national pride and the present situation of China, isolated within the socialist camp and banned from the United Nations, do not exactly favour this solution which, nevertheless, seems the wisest as evidenced by the fact that businessmen, stimulated by my lectures on *Babélien*, recently recognized that my proposal "at first glance bold, even extravagant, is very interesting. A more detailed examination of this proposal shows that it would indeed offer definite advantages; still, a question remains; does it really have any chance of being accepted?"[7]

Was it really such a "bold" proposal? What did I do except take over, in a form hardly changed, an idea which Descartes expressed to Father Mersenne, in a letter of November, 1629, where-

---

[7] *Bureau* (September, 1962), 21.

after expounding all the inconveniences of an artificial universal language, he says:

> Thus, all the usefulness I can see as resulting from this invention (the invention of an universal language) is for writing: namely, that he (Mr. Hardy) had a large dictionary printed with all the languages in which he would like to be understood, and assigned to each basic word common characters corresponding to the meaning and not to the syllables, as an identical character for *aimer, amare* and φιλεῖν (*philein*): and those who would have these dictionaries and know its grammar could, by looking for all these characters one after the other, interpret in their own language those which should be written. But that system would be good only to read mysteries and revelations; as far as other things are concerned, to go to the trouble of looking up all the words in a dictionary, would mean that one did not have much else to do, and thus I do not see this system to be of much use.

Like Descartes, I am distrustful of this *metalanguage*, even though, I know, as he did, it could be realized:

> Now, I believe strongly that this language is possible, and that it is possible for us to find the science on which it depends, by means of which peasants would be able to judge the truth of things better than philosophers are now doing. But do not hope ever to see it in use! It presupposes great changes in the order of things, and it would be necessary for the whole world to be nothing but an earthly paradise, which is worth proposing only in fiction.

In between the universal language of the esperanto or volapuk type, and the metalanguage of an earthly paradise, Descartes thus foresaw a *universal writing form*. Leibniz, on the other hand, knew that the signs inferred by Descartes exist and answer the needs of his times: Chinese ideographs, each of which expresses a concept and which everyone can, according to his own desire, *pronounce* in his own language, as long as he knows the *meaning* of the characters. Thus, the idea seems to me rather obvious, but I also recognize, as does the editor of the *Bureau*, that it has little chance, even today, of being accepted. What other solution remains, in this case, except the translating machine? This is the solution to which our businessmen are turning; I have said why we comparatists cannot adopt it.

So, here we are, in the middle of an unsolved problem!

III

OBJECTIVES, METHODS, PROGRAMS

Assuming that this apparently insoluble problem is solved, what should be the objectives, and consequently the method or methods, and the programs of comparative literature? For three quarters of a century, enough has been written on this subject to fill the library of the average educated man; let us add a few pages to it, if only to bring to light the lessons of the Congresses held in 1958 in Chapel Hill, and in 1962 in Budapest.[8]

The Two "Schools"

For want of an American visa, I was much too late in getting to Chapel Hill where I had been invited by my American colleagues and awarded a travel fellowship by the Ford Foundation. I regretted all the more this encroachment of the political domain on the cultural since, had I been able to read at the meeting the paper I had prepared, the opposition which became obvious between comparatists of the "American school" and of the "French school" would have been less brutal; and Mrs. Nieoupakoïeva would have had less reason to profess that, year after year, the line of demarcation was becoming clearer and the gap deeper between the American and French conceptions.

That the two "schools"—or tendencies rather—are in disagreement, no one would deny. It would be an oversimplification, however, to consider the French school as a unit, an orthodoxy. No mind is more open than that of Marcel Bataillon who is presently directing the *Revue de littérature comparée*. Eager to make clear the direction he intended to give to his editorial policy, he created an editorial committee including not only Frenchmen as diver-

[8] Reports, papers, and discussions were published *in extenso* in 1963, under the auspices of the Hungarian Academy of Sciences.

gent as Marie-Jeanne Durry, Jean Sarrailh, Jean Pommier, Henri Roddier, Jacques Voisine, Jean Fabre, and Robert Escarpit, but also various representatives from abroad: Gustave Charlier, Werner P. Friederich, Helmut Hatzfeld, Carlo Pelligrini, Franco Simone, and Fritz Schalk. Could he have more discreetly suggested that the French school does not ignore foreign schools, not even the American school? By surprising me, in accepting me as a member of this committee, was he not suggesting that all the interpretations of our discipline should henceforth be expressed in the pages of the review? As Voisine expressed it recently in an issue of *Hikaku Bungaku*, "comparative literature is practiced with ample diversity in the different chairs existing in France. It is opening new horizons: Slavic countries and the Orient are beginning to attract researchers. We would show little faith in comparative studies if we did not congratulate ourselves on this diversity and if we sought to denounce the lack of orthodoxy in the new methods being tried here and there." Several persons believing I am the one guilty of "a lack of orthodoxy," though I am not openly condemned (which Henry H. H. Remak confirms in his way when he refers to me as the *enfant terrible* of French comparatism or suggests that "the appointment of a *rebel*, René Etiemble, to the chair of comparative literature at the Sorbonne, a chair formerly occupied by Jean-Marie Carré, is a sign of some significance"), I would like to make it clear, therefore, that I am speaking for myself and not as a spokesman for my French colleagues.[9]

During the Chapel Hill Congress, in 1958, this crisis in comparative literature manifested itself often in the form of innuendos, sometimes even vehemently. What was suspected by those who, by profession, read both the *Revue de littérature comparée* and *Comparative Literature*, became obvious to those others who, because of a generously conciliatory mind, were trying to ignore the fact that comparatists are still at the stage of discussing the objec-

[9] Henry H. H. Remak, "Comparative Literature at the Crossroads: Diagnosis, Therapy and Prognosis," *Yearbook of Comparative and General Literature*, IX (1960). The appendix contains an extensive bibliography dealing with the "crisis" of our discipline.

tive of their work and the methods it requires. I am thinking especially of the Japanese, anxious to maintain a balance between the American and French conceptions: influenced at first by the doctrine of Van Tieghem and French comparatism—and here how can one underestimate the role played by Koyabayashi or Kinji Shimada?—the Japanese, especially from 1954 on, were disturbed, not without justification, by what is sometimes called the "positivism" of the French method and its "historicism." Saburo Ota subsequently subscribed to the theses of René Wellek, one of the theorists of the "American school."

Historicism and Criticism

Yes, despite the efforts of the conciliators, today, throughout the world, comparative literature is divided, and at times, torn between several tendencies, two of which at least have little sympathy for each other. One, which maintains that this discipline, virtually contemporaneous with historical studies (to such an extent that Montesquieu and Voltaire, in as much as they were interested in history, seem, at the same time, to have laid down some principles of comparative literature), must be, and furthermore can be, nothing else but a branch of literary history, the latter understood in the most "*événementiel*" (factual) sense of the word, as they say today, or the most anecdotal, as I would say. The other tendency considers that even though two literatures have not had historical relations, it is legitimate to compare the literary genres which each developed for its own use. "Even when the possibility of direct influence is ruled out," to borrow the words of Professor James Hightower, who teaches Chinese literature at Harvard, comparative literature remains not only possible, but in fact singularly stimulating.

Historicists

In one camp are grouped those who imagine they are, or pretend to be, applying to comparative literature the historical method of Lanson, but who almost always forget the essence of it, to wit, that for the founder of the most orthodox literary history, the historical method, far from constituting the essence of the teaching of literature, could, and was supposed in fact to constitute only an approach to it. This is clearly stated in Lanson's well-known *Histoire de la littérature française* which dominated our teaching for half a century, but whose purposes, alas, have been ill understood. Does one ever read prefaces? This one, however, well deserves to be thought over:

> I do not conceive, therefore, that one studies literature for any other reason than to cultivate oneself, and for any other reason than because one enjoys it. Undoubtedly, those who intend to become teachers must systematize their knowledge, submit their study to methods, and direct it towards more precise (I will say more scientific, if they want) notions than mere *amateurs* of letters need do. But one should never lose sight of two things: one, that he who will not first of all work to develop in his students a taste for literature will be a bad teacher of literature . . . ; another, that no one will know how to give his teaching this effectiveness if, before being a scholar, he is not himself an *amateur*.

You are reading correctly, "*before being a scholar.*" *Amateur* of poems, thus Jean Prévost defined himself, Prévost, this humanist who translated not only Spanish, English, German, and Modern Greek poems, but also, with the help of a Chinese man of letters and inferior French translations, Chinese poems. *L'Amateur de poèmes*, one of Prévost's most brilliant books, ranks him high among the good interpreters, that is to say, the good servants of comparative literature, and that, because, faithful to Lanson's requirements, this writer who defended at Lyons, during the last war, a noted and remarkable thesis on *La Création chez Stendhal* was *mad* (as he writes himself) about some Chinese poets.

In the usurped name of Lansonism, the least gifted and consequently the most obstinate epigones of the old master, lived for half a century as if his postulate were null and void: for them, the most vain bibliographical compilations, the anecdote, the accessory, constituted the essential of the work of the comparatist, the only work, at any rate, which fell within their province. Certain representatives of the French school mechanically applied to comparative literature this caricature of the Lanson method; whereas in Lanson's mind, historical, honest, and precise researches were the prelude to literary study, to the enjoyment of the works (and guaranteed at the same time the *amateur* against cavalier criticism, of the kind which Jules Lemaître and many other literary journalists afforded, at that time, brilliant but distressing examples), these zealots presumed to circumscribe literary study, even comparative literature, to historical work. Yet, shortly before his death, even a master as keen as Jean-Marie Carré when he agreed to preface Marius-François Guyard's *Littérature comparée*, committed the same mistake. Anxious to demarcate, after Baldensperger and Van Tieghem, the province of our discipline, did he not define, in these terms, what we must indeed call orthodoxy *à la française*:

> Comparative literature is a branch of literary history: it is the study of international spiritual relations, relations of fact which existed between Byron and Pushkin, Goethe and Carlyle, Walter Scott and Vigny, between the works, inspirations, and even lives of writers belonging to several literatures.
>
> It does not essentially consider works in their original value, but it is especially concerned with how nations and writers transform what they have borrowed. . . . Finally, comparative literature is not the "General Literature" which is taught in the United States. It can lead to it eventually; and for some, it must do so. But these large parallelisms (and synchronisms also) such as humanism, classicism, romanticism, realism, symbolism, risk, by being too systematic, too far extended in space and time, being dissipated into abstraction, arbitrariness, and mere labels. Though it can lead the way to such syntheses, comparative literature cannot produce them.

Not that all of this appears to me to deserve criticism. In order to reduce these concepts to absurdity (but after all, these are, very often, concepts invented or systematized by historians of literature), when I taught a course in pre-romanticism in Europe at the end of the 18th century, at the University of Montpellier, after gathering from the textbooks of our historians all the themes suitable for cataloguing, *la nature, le paysage-état d'âme, l'amour-passion, la fatalité, la sensibilité, le temps qui passe, les ruines,* in a word, everything, I gave a course that could not have been more orthodox, and concluded with these words: "I want to point out that all my quotations on the birth of pre-romanticism in Europe were taken from Chinese poets, from K'iu Yuan, who lived before the Christian era, to the epoch of the Song." Thus, I was justifying the prudence of Jean-Marie Carré, and with the same underhanded blow, those who consider that the history of the *relations of fact* between writers, schools, or literary genres, does not exhaust our discipline. For, if I am able to throw light on all the themes of European pre-romanticism in the 18th century with quotations taken from Chinese poetry prior to the Christian era and from the first twelve centuries of the Christian era, it is obviously because there exist forms, genres, invariables, in a word, that man exists, and so does literature.

The Critics

Indeed, they are not wrong, those who, like René Wellek in the United States and many others elsewhere, think that the study of the history of comparative literatures does not coincide with the comparative study of literatures, that literatures are the systems of forms which man adds to his natural language, and that the comparative study of literatures, instead of limiting itself to the study of *relations of facts,* must attempt to lead to the consideration of the value of the works, even lead to, why not? value judgments, perhaps even, and in my opinion, contribute to the elaboration of values in a way somewhat less arbitrary than those by which we now live or because of which we are in jeopardy.

With Jean-Marie Carré, I believe that, since it is still at present in its infancy, comparative literature cannot identify itself with either Goethe's *Weltliteratur* or with the *General Literature* of the United States, neither in fact with that World Literature of which, my Soviet colleague Anissimov was telling me recently, a history is being prepared by the Moscow Academy of Sciences; but I do believe that it must lead us to it. I agree with René Wellek that comparative literature condemns itself to lasting unfulfillment unless the ultimate objective of historical studies, which the French and Soviet scholars have reason to value, is to enable us to speak, at long last, of individual *literatures*, even of general literature, aesthetics, and rhetoric. For Guillermo de Torre is fully justified in wondering if, among all the disciplines practiced today, the one which corresponds most closely with what Goethe had in mind when he spoke of *Weltliteratur*, is not comparative literature: "Si el unico territorio que se acerque al dominio entrevisto de la Welt-literature no seria el de la literatura comparada." ("I wonder if the only field which comes close to the province envisioned as *Welt-literatur* would not be that of comparative literature.") It is under-standable that, because it suggests the idea of generality, that is to say, approximation, the expression "general literature" frightens the meticulous historians. But who can fail to understand the corre-sponding misgivings of Marcel Bataillon, when he objects to the expression: "Comparison," he writes, "is only one of the methods of what we call, by a name which suggests rather badly what it means, comparative literature. Often I tell myself that general literature would be a better expression, and then, I immediately see the disadvantages which would follow the adoption of a new term and which would bring to mind generalities and no longer concrete relations between living works."

"Donner un sens plus pur aux mots de la tribu"

Since the most illustrious of French comparatists raises doubts about the very name of our discipline, they are not wrong—and they are, moreover, numerous—those who insist that the first task of comparative literature today should be to define the words it uses, and, first of all, to define itself. At the very moment when Western European comparatists plan to prepare and publish a technical vocabulary of our discipline, in which the meaning of the words most often and often also least judiciously used, would be elucidated from a historical point of view, it is good to learn that the Congress of Comparative Literature organized in Budapest under the auspices of the Academies of Science of the socialist countries, proposed to its sections three subjects for consideration: 1) present problems of comparative literature; 2) formation and transformation of terms used in literary history; 3) historical and comparative examination of Eastern European literatures: is it possible and necessary to prepare a comparative history of these literatures? The first section examined the objects and the methods of our discipline, the second insisted rightfully on one of the tasks upon which its future will be dependent. Who would be in a better position than the comparatist to know that, as soon as we enter the realm of the abstract, the concepts of a given language only rarely coincide with those of another language? Rather, they overlap, each being composed of parts of several foreign concepts, and the latter varying with the language in question: in German, *Volk* is charged with an affective and racial meaning which does not inhere in our term *peuple*. *Völkisch* does not mean *populaire* at all, but rather adds to *rassisch*, a quasi-scientific notion which can be translated by *racial*, a romantic and leftist nuance which did not prevent it from deviating toward the monstrously normative meaning of *raciste* under the Nazi influence. Historically, German classicism has few traits in common with French classicism. Aesthetically, however, they do possess some characteristics in common. How can one explain historically that all the themes of European pre-romanticism are found, as I have mentioned, in ancient China and the China of the T'ang? Yet, aesthetically, the analogies force themselves into consideration. Thus, we will have to decide whether the term *romanticism* is, in this case, legitimate or not.

And when we come to a word such as *realism*, and its substitutes: *critical realism, social realism*, we are faced with a mystery. Whether they belong, ideologically, to the socialist or to the capitalist world, the specialists have been quarrelling for the past thirty years about the meaning of these words. With the end of Zhdanovism, perhaps it will be possible, some day, to see them reach an agreement. This was the way it looked in Budapest: when some professors expressed reservations about Lukacs, it was to deplore in him the theorist who too strongly contrasted Balzac and Tolstoi —the only worthy realists—with the naturalist Zola (which reminds me of the brilliant parallel which the Hungarian critic revealed to me some thirty years ago: the horse race in *Anna Karenina* and in *Nana*; naturalism was roundly condemned while realism was approved); moreover, some East German and Polish comparatists recognized that the word *realism* had been abused, distorted, and emptied of all meaning. The speech which Louis Aragon had just delivered in Prague was perhaps not unrelated to this happy reversal: since Louis Aragon who, in 1935, had established the dogmas of *social realism* in Western Europe, proposed in 1962, a reconsideration which does him honor, one can imagine, without being naïve, that the comparatists of the whole world will soon be able to reach an agreement as to the meaning which this word should be given.

The reports of Voisine, Professor at the University of Lille, on the history and the meaning of the term *autobiography*, and of Brahmer, member of the Warsaw Academy of Sciences, on the use of the term *mannerism* in literary history, were inspired by the same judicious concern.

In order to serve our discipline well, it is necessary, therefore, to endow it, first of all, with a precise vocabulary having a universal meaning. In the event that, despite the present trend of thought, agreement about all terms could not be reached by the socialist and capitalist worlds (which I would find unfortunate, if not dangerous), the least one can expect and which must be required is a dictionary such as Lalande's philosophical dictionary, which would express with honesty all the meanings that one finds for each and every word: a *vocabulary* which, under the heading *realism* would give the various interpretations of this concept, according to whether it is used by critics of the conservative bourgeoisie of the 19th century, by the critics of the liberal bourgeoisie of the 20th century, by the critics who claim allegiance to Marx, or by those who bow to Zhdanov.

Such a dictionary would permit one to verify that history and historicism are not always progressive, nor aesthetics always reactionary; it would help to develop a comparative literature which, combining the historical method with the critical spirit, archive research with the *explications de textes*, the prudence of the sociologist with the boldness of the aesthetician, would at last, at one stroke, give our discipline a worthy purpose and appropriate methods.

Domain of the Comparatist "à la Française"

In examining the topics which Guyard expounds in his small volume of popularization, it is regrettable that they steer us away from literature itself: Guyard invites the comparatist to study the agents of literary cosmopolitanism, that is to say, the works of men who, at a given time, contribute to the dissemination of foreign letters in a given country. Next, he considers the fortunes of literary genres, provided that each be well defined and considered in "a recipient milieu clearly defined in time and space." Then he takes the careers of themes, such as the *Stoffgeschichte* of the *vergleichende Literaturwissenschaft* (and God knows that from Gendarme de Bévotte's *Don Juan* to Charles Dédéyan's *Faust*, the French school has taken advantage of this franchise!); the careers of authors; and the foreign sources of individuals and schools. Finally, he discusses the image which one country forms of another country (ever since Ascoli's work *La Grande Bretagne devant l'opinion française*, 1927, this kind of research also prospers in France, almost as much as the studies of Icelandic travellers in Madagascar, Malagasy travellers in Kamchatka, or Swedish travellers in Bangkok!).

If, for every valuable study, twenty mediocre accounts of travels in Patagonia or Labrador were to be published, by inept Italian or Russian writers, would one's understanding of a work of literature *as such* be increased one iota? Travelogues, even the worst written ones, interest the historian, the geographer, the sociologist. They are also of interest to those of us who are concerned with the movement of ideas. But I would not claim that this kind of study, to which I devoted several years of my life, is, in the strictest sense of the term, comparative literature. As for the unavoidably false idea that the French create for themselves about the United States through reading the dramatic and romantic literature published since the Civil War, or the caricature image that these same Frenchmen acquire about Japan or Turkey, through Pierre Loti's novels, is that a question of literature? Here again, these works are mainly the concern of the historian, the sociologist, or the statesman.

For and Against the "Stoffgeschichte"

Paul Hazard, as even Guyard admits "would have willingly forbidden to the comparatist the study of themes: they are indeed only the matter of literature; literature begins only when themes acquire value, thanks to genre, form, and style." The historical study of themes remains nevertheless one of the favorite subjects of the so-called French school. One of the works I have recently received, Roland Derche's *Quatre mythes poétiques: Oedipe, Narcisse, Psyché, Lorelei,* treats of four poetic myths in certain works in several literatures. Provided it is based upon a minute study of precise texts, the study of a theme can be useful in the understanding of literature (as well as to sociology and even religious sociology, in addition to history). Witness the recent work of Robert Vivier, Professor at the University of Liège, an accomplished Romance scholar who, starting from poems he sensitively explicates, shows the evolution of the theme of Icarus through literature. A poet as much as a professor, Robert Vivier knows how to reconcile the methods of history with the requirements of taste. The historian will be happy to find out that the young Icarus who, despite the advice of his dad Dedalus, wanted to be clever, was at first condemned for his disobedience; only later was he exalted at the expense of his father (who is no longer remembered except through the name of an inextricable labyrinth). At first, the architect Dedalus was, and rightly so, the great man; yet, when Arthur Lundkvist wants today to glorify the god Rimbaud, he enthusiastically writes *Ikarus flykt* (Stockholm, 1939), while in 1954, writers vie more than ever with one another in comparing Rimbaud with that little fool Icarus, as for example, Luc Estang who calls *"Rimbaud-Icare"* in his *Tombeau de Rimbaud ("Tout est Icare!")*. Today, "it's all Icarus," alas! A study such as Robert Vivier's can thus enlighten us with respect to contemporary poetry. But if this writer had not interspersed his work with careful translations and explanations, he would have provided us with an essay on sociology, not with a work in comparative *literatures*. I will never claim that my dissertation studies, *Le Mythe de Rimbaud*, represent the ideal of our discipline. They are sociological essays, even essays dealing with religious sociology, which only seldom touch upon comparative literature. The third volume, on which I am still working, will, here and there, conform more closely to the ideal of our specialty which I am here proposing.

I would say the same with regard to almost all of what is being written in France under the official title of comparative literature. When, for example, our specialists study genres, they confine themselves to considering only "the comparative history of literary genres," that is, the "relations of fact" between, let us say, Spanish drama and the French theater, the *commedia dell'arte* and Molière's farce, the English "Gothic" novel and its French counterparts.

The Ideal Comparatist

Let me be clearly understood! I do not intend to rule the historical discipline out of our training. We are "embarked," as the fellow says: history presses on us on all sides, oppresses us, and often crushes us. I find it reasonable, and even necessary, for all comparatists to study, from the historical point of view, at least one period in which the *relations of fact* did play decided roles. I want my comparatist to be well trained in the examination of archives and collections of little magazines. Besides the training of a historian, I also wish him to have the training of a sociologist.

I would not even forbid him general culture. He should have, in addition, more than a smattering of knowledge of the plastic arts and the music of the period he has chosen to make his own! In these times of excessive specialization, it is fitting that one discipline at least—ours—should recognize the importance of what as a sacrifice to the demon of the century is sometimes today called the *"sciences diagonales"* (cross-fertilizing sciences), and what, in my youth, was still called general culture, or even more modestly, culture. Yes, I wish our comparatist to be as learned as possible; I even wish him to have the ambition of an encyclopedist, the ambition of a Diderot. It was not by chance that two men who, in the 18th century, participated in the philosophical movement, Montesquieu and Voltaire, were led to sense, and were even able to formulate some of the precepts and principles of our discipline. In his *Essai sur la poésie épique*, Voltaire tried to isolate the elements which belong essentially to the epic—to wit, a single action, simple, great, and interesting—from these elements: the choice of episodes, the nature of the marvelous, the intervention of such or such celestial power, which can change according to the character of each nation, the accidents of history, and the fantasy of the author. In the same judicious spirit, Montesquieu started from the tonic accent of such and such a language in order to deduce the characters proper to the poetry of such and such a linguistic domain: this language requiring preferably iambic or iambico-anapestic metrics, that one trochaic or dactylic metrics. As for encyclopedists (I know some in various disciplines and in the 20th century), I would like them to be more numerous in our field. If he does not have the encyclopedic vocation, no one is forced by any law that I know of to become a comparatist.

I also want our comparatist to be a man of taste and pleasure. I want all his preliminary studies to be for him only the means to read texts with more intelligence and consequently with more pleasure and more delight than those who know little or nothing. I want him to be an *amateur* of poems, or the theater, or novels, as Lanson wanted his historian of letters to be. Thus we must consider as promising the 1958 Chapel Hill Congress, where several scholars of the "American school," repeating the ideas expounded many times on the pages of *Comparative Literature*, vigorously rehabilitated criticism, too often neglected by French comparatists. No more than I does René Wellek forget that in *Comparative Literature* there is the word *comparative*, but no more than I does he believe that the other word, *literature*, should be forgotten.[10]

Which does not mean that I would approve of several Americans who, under the cover of pure, or so-called pure, criticism, reject anything that might look like what they contemptuously call "positivist" experience in our discipline. Using the excuse that literature is a product of the human imagination, some assert that it cannot be, if we are to believe them, the object of analysis. If Malone, for example, limited himself to ridiculing those who, under the pretext of studying sources and influences, pile up an historical or sociological jumble which explains nothing at all, I would be in full accord with him! No study of sources will ever explain why the sheep is transformed, as the case may be, into a lion, a tiger, or a panther, or even a multi-colored rock python. But when the condemnation of "positivism" leads to pure aestheticism, I am suspicious, for I maintain that aesthetics has everything to gain from precise studies, as we see from the second Congress of Aesthetics and Sciences of Art, which was held in Paris in 1937.[11] For the near future, the comparatist at his best would be the one who, endowed with an encyclopedic bent, and familiar with several of the most important languages which will be written in the world around the year 2000, would also have an intimate experience of literary beauty. With various success, Baldensperger, Jean-Marie Carré, and Paul Hazard have tried their hands at non-scholarly works: Fernand Baldensperger attempted poetry, Jean-Marie Carré, travel books; and Paul Hazard confided to me long ago that he had wanted to write (and had even published) novels; in the case of Robert Vivier, the poet is worthy of the teacher. If Marcel Bataillon towers above French comparatism today, he does not owe this

---

[10] See my *Hygiène des lettres*, III (Paris: Gallimard, 1958).
[11] Second Congress of Aesthetics and History of Art: Paris, 1937; 2 vols. (Alcan, 1937).

stature to his knowledge alone; his interpretations of *Celestina* and of *Viaje de Turquía* are those of an artist.

Literature is Made with Words . . .

If *mad* love for letters or experience in creation are lacking, one can at least require the comparatist to have good taste. Literature being made with words, with sentences, with paragraphs, with chapters, scenes, acts, lines, strophes, and anti-strophes, comparative literature will have to become interested in words, their interrelations and, when the case applies, the extent to which they are affected by words and structures borrowed from other languages. Each language has its own genius, but, ever since there have been men on the earth, languages have affected one another. Why, then, is comparatism neglecting this interaction and the advantages (or disadvantages) resulting from it as far as literatures are concerned? In the 16th century, our humanists had to struggle against the "Hellenisation" and "Italianisation" of the French language. In the 18th century, Jose de Cadalso, in his *Cartas Marruecas*, wittily ridiculed his *afrancesados* compatriots. In the 20th century, Argentine, Peruvian, or Mexican chroniclers of the language condemn the gallicisms which once again infest and contaminate Spanish. In our day, the widespread influence of the press and television (and in the future the influence of universal television) is dangerously modifying the structure of languages and the nature of their relations. Without falling into chauvinism and nationalism, which hardly becomes us, we have the right, as Mrs. Nieoupakoïeva declared in Budapest, to wish that comparative literature would help us better to understand and (why not?) better to defend each of our literatures. If only to safeguard each of the various literatures in maintaining its own essential being, the massive interaction of languages one upon another, American on French, French and American on German, etc., deserve studies in depth. When Enver Esenkova published in Istanbul in 1959, *Turk dilinde Fransiz tesiri*, in which he examines the phonetic, morphological, and semantic influences of French on the Turkish lexicon since the 16th century, he is engaged in comparative literature, and far more precisely so indeed than those who are attempting to find out if such a French writer really had a mistress from Berlin and what German *"gestes"* she taught him.

Therefore, I do not believe I failed comparatism in devoting several years of my life and three years of lecturing at the Sorbonne to the study of that French variety of the contemporary *Babélien* which I have christened the *sabir atlantique*. We are dealing here with a fact of colonization.

Our century being, however, the century of decolonization, it will be important to examine the extent to which the languages of the colonizing powers have acted upon the languages and literatures of the colonized countries; and *vice-versa*, the extent to which the languages of the colonies have reacted upon the oppressors. All kinds of countries having for a long time endured colonial status, the study of bilingualism as it affects the creation of literary works should be the order of the day, and not only from the statistical, psychological and pedagogical points of view.

Comparative Stylistics are too much Neglected

Literature being made with words and sentences, insufficient study is devoted, in my opinion, to what should be the very foundation of our studies: comparative stylistics. Fortunately, at the same time that general stylistics was regaining the favor of university people, this sub-discipline won in France disciples who were able to apply it to comparative literature. A collection of studies in comparative stylistics has just begun publication in the Didier Editions with two valuable volumes.[12] At about the same time, Boleslaw Kielski published in Łódź, *Struktura języków francuskiego i polskiego świetle analizy porównawczej (Comparative Study of*

---

[12] J.-P. Vinay and J. Darbelnet, *Stylistique comparée du français et de l'anglais* (Paris: Didier, 1958); Alfred Malblanc, *Stylistique comparée du français et de l'allemand* (Paris: Didier, 1961). See also Gilbert Barth's research on "la fréquence et la valeur des parties du discours en français, en anglais et en espagnol."

French and Polish from the Stylistic Point of View). Let us hope that such works multiply and that they will not be abandoned to linguists who are lacking at times in sensitivity to beautiful language. The comparatists of the socialist world particularly excel in comparative stylistics—I have especially in mind Alexeiev and Jirmounski—so that comparative literature seems to be on the right track. Let us make sure that it stays on it!

... and Comparative Metrics ...

Poetry being made of verses, stanzas, and cantos, it is proper for us deliberately to direct our students towards work in comparative metrics and prosody. When I read, recently, László Kardos's work on Hungarian rhyme (*Betrachtungen über den ungarischen Reim*[13]), or a few among those of László Gáldi (*Essai d'une interprétation fonctionnelle du vers. Une analyse de stylistique littéraire: le sonnet "Afara-i-Toamna" de M. Eminescou, Une strophe, ses métamorphoses et son expressivité de Goethe à Eminescou; Les variétés de l'accent dans le vers russe;* and *Un grand disciple roumain de J. Kochanowski: le métropolite Dosithée*), I realized more than ever how far our Javanese travellers in Peru or Peruvian travellers in Java are from the core of our discipline. Used with delicacy, comparative phonetics should help us better to understand the quality of the poems we are considering. While reading Louis Michel's dissertation, *Etude du son 's' en latin et en roman* (the subtitle is, *De la phonétique au style*), how could I have failed to remember the poet André Spire's work *Plaisir poétique et plaisir musculaire*? How could I have failed to wish that our students become closely concerned with those questions of comparative poetics? Therefore, I entrusted several of them with the task of studying, for example, the influence of the French free verse on Hungarian poetry, Russian poetry, Chinese poetry, and Vietnamese poetry in the 20th century. I await the one who will treat this subject with respect to Japanese poetry.

[13] *Acta Litteraria*, IV (Budapest, 1961), 207-223.

. . . and the Comparative Study of Images . . .

Images are no less important in the poem that euphony, rhyme, and rhythm. How enriching would the comparative study of poetic images be! For want of being initiated in this discipline the Western reader will be misled by the images of the Chinese poets. See the introduction of Paul Demiéville to his *Anthologie de la poésie chinoise classique*:[14] "White signifies for us purity; for the Chinese, it is the color of mourning, and evokes sadness, coldness, solitude, as for example, in an expression such as *white moon*." In a poem of Li Yu, there is a reference to a western pavillion. Why western? Because the subject of the poem is autumn and melancholy. "On the other hand, in ancient times, the West was the part of the house reserved to the wife, who belongs to the *yin*, principle of shade and dampness; the mention, in such a context, of an eastern pavillion would to the Chinese reader create a false note." A hundred Chinese images will thus be the sources of as many misunderstandings. Demiéville offers us a perfect example of such a misunderstanding: "The flower of the lotus, whose roots soak in the vase, but which raises its large immaculate corolla above the surface of the water, is, in Buddhism . . . the transcendent purity of the Saint; Judith Gautier, in her *Livre de Jade*, misunderstands when she shows us a poet making a declaration of love to a lotus."

How illuminating it would be to study, in particular, the images of profane and sacred love; to isolate those governed by the climate, fauna, flora, way of life, and historical and other accidents, the very nature of the language (plays on and with words), and those which are preserved in all civilizations, all languages, constituting something similar to the invariables of the human imagination. When in exalting the beauty of women, the Tamil poet praises their "*yeux de poisson*" (fish-like eyes), he is probably recapturing a vision of the eyes illustrated by the painting of upper Egypt and which reappears even in more than one of Cocteau's drawings, and in at least one of Colette's novels. At the same time, he reveals that he

[14] Paris: Gallimard, 1962, in the series "Connaissance de l'Orient."

belongs to a fishing civilization. Association in France with the expression "*oeil de poisson frit*" (fried fish eye), the Tamil eye must disconcert us when a poet proposes it to us for the first time. Still, it will eventually appear pleasing to us. When exalting a woman's breasts, the author, whoever he was, of those "scandalous" *Jeoup'ou-t'ouan* compares them to "*deux oeufs sortis du ventre d'une poule et qu'on ferait éclater en appuyant dessus*," (two eggs freshly out of a hen's belly, which would burst when one pressed down on them), I am afraid he thoroughly discourages the French reader, since the image of "fried eggs, sunny side up," rather than an aphrodisiac would be, to him, an anaphrodisiac. When the Chinese poet evokes love with images of war, siege, strategy, horse and rider, garden and flower stands, shoe and shoe-tree, goat and stake, sea-like movements of mingled lovers, we feel at ease and at home. Could it be that we are here confronted with what, in the expression of the sentiment of love, corresponds to what must be called human nature?

. . . and the Art of Translation . . .

The understanding of poetry and the art of translation being of great concern to our discipline, I would like to see our students, instead of being led astray into pseudo-sociological studies such as the Russian mirage in American literature or the American image in Russian literature, directed toward the comparative study of translations.[15] Whether one studies the various English translations of a single poem of Saint-John Perse, or the various French translations of a single poem of Tóth Árpád or of Vörösmarty, or whether one examines the translations of the same poem in three, four, five, ten languages with different phonetics and structures, in all cases one will really be engaged in comparative literature. As long as the method of the *explication de textes* is applied tactfully, the comparative study of translations allows us to penetrate in

[15] See the excellent study by Edmond Gary, "Pour une théorie de la traduction," *Diogène*, No. 40 (1962), 96-120, which also includes a bibliography of recent works on this subject.

depth the art of the poet; to isolate in each poem what belongs to themes and ideas expressible in prose and what belongs to the gifts and conquests of poetry; to define which parts of this poetry are transmissible; and to discover what is lost in one language and kept in another. It sometimes happens that the translation helps in understanding the original, or that, better than the original, betrays it. Goethe is said to have understood fully all he had incorporated into his *Faust* only after reading Nerval's translation! About 20 years ago, in a learned journal some passages of the German text were explained, thanks to French interpretations. When the comparatist wonders how to adapt the *explication de textes* to our discipline, when he errs to the extent that he suggests that candidates explain simultaneously three texts written in three different languages, each of which describes the forest, the desert or the sea, why does he not realize that it would be better instead to apply oneself to various translations of the same work? Such would be, in my opinion, the finished model of comparative *explication*.

. . . and Structure . . .

A literary work is, finally, a structured whole, fitting more or less one of the genres among which the writer divides his activity. Our comparatists have, of course, studied genres, but only in as much as they are Western genres connected by *relations of fact*. Granted, it is important that this kind of work be continued. It would be fallacious, however, to limit the comparison of genres to this kind of study. Let us give two examples: after the Meiji Revolution, 19th century Europe became infatuated with Japan, and, at the beginning of the 20th century, it tried to adapt certain genres of Japanese poetry to German, Spanish, and French. Claudel published some would-be *dodoitsu*, and *haiku* flowered in Europe. It remains to be seen whether poems published under this name still deserve an *"appellation"* which the cheese and wine merchant would call *"contrôlée"* or a *"marque"* (trade name) which the manufacturers of socks and brassieres would call *"déposée"* (registered).

When they read those of our would-be *haiku* which strive for the conciseness of the original, the Japanese I know find in them nothing like theirs. Does this deception depend on economic or political conditions? On philosophical or religious super-structures? On traditional imagery? On phonetics, on syntax? When, furthermore, one knows that the *haiku* consists of 17 syllables and that there happens to be a Frenchman, Victor Paul d'Arsent, who published *Haikais à la manière occidentale*,[16] a collection of poems some of which are two pages long, one wonders whether it is permissible in this case to use the Japanese word. Here is a case where the study of genres and their employment in a foreign milieu is in fact founded, according to the requirements of the French school, on *relations of fact*. Another example: in China, between the 5th and the 18th centuries, starting from the hagiographic themes of Buddhism preached in the spoken language to convert masses, a whole literature of realist and magical short stories was created, the *siao chouo*, which, uniting, working on, and influencing one another, produced little by little the great Chinese novels (*Hong-leou mong, Kin-p'ing-mei*, etc.) which flourished at the time when, in Europe, bringing together the picaresque of Spain, the libertinage of the *Decameron*, the beauty of the *Novelas ejemplares*, there appeared *Gil Blas, Tom Jones, Moll Flanders*, and a score of other novels whose technique, tone and spirit shockingly resemble what, sheltered from any Western influence, was being elaborated in China. Certainly, over there as in the West, the vogue of the novel seems to coincide with the flowering of a bourgeois or merchant class; but who would claim that the European novel, like the Chinese novel, sprang from Buddhist preaching?

And how is it that Chinese novelists give to their masterpieces the very forms adopted by the 18th century European novelists? A systematic study of the novels produced by those civilizations most alien to ours (the *Gengi Monogatari* of the Japanese, the *Shilappadikaram* of the Tamils, the *Kim Van Kiêu* of the Vietnamese) would perhaps bring to light and make obvious, on the one hand, the permanent elements of the genre of the "romance,"

[16] Avignon: Les Presses universelles, 1957-1958.

those elements without which there can be no novel, and on the other hand, those constituent parts of the genre which result, more or less arbitrarily, from historical circumstances. Here is a case where the study of genres is not founded upon *relations of fact* of an historical order. Will we say, then, that this is not legitimate?

As far as I am concerned, I do not understand how a European comparatist who pretends to be interested in drama can refuse to study the *Noh* and the *Traités secrets* of Zeami Motokiyo, with the excuse that, until the 20th century, the *Noh* had not influenced the French stage. James Liu seems to me most alert to these considerations in his book, published in London in 1955, *Elizabethan and Yuan: A Brief Comparison of Some Conventions in Poetic Drama.*[17] Although the Yuan theater did not influence the Elizabethan stage, this study, albeit too much of a summary and needing further elaboration, is indeed a legitimate comparative study, in the precise meaning of the term, in which it is already possible to notice that between these two dramaturgies there exist several singular and notable similarities which, in addition, show them both to be in sharp contrast to the kind of theater which knows only how to present "a slice of life, as lived by Mr. Smith or Mr. Jones in his drawing room with the fourth wall missing."

From Comparative Literature to Comparative Poetry

By combining the two methods which consider themselves diametrically opposed but which, in fact, must complement each other—the historical inquiry and the critical or aesthetic reflection —comparative literature would then be irresistibly drawn towards comparative poetry. Since, instead of being deduced from metaphysical principles, it would be induced from meticulous research, either on the historical evolution of genres or on the nature and structure of each of the forms created for each genre in the different civilizations, this aesthetics, hostile to all dogmatism, could be

[17] China Society Occasional Papers, edited by S. Howard Hansford, No. 8 (London: The China Society, 1955).

of genuine utility. We know that great works always surprise us by an air of novelty. However infatuated we may be with aesthetics, who among us would dream of imposing his own rhetoric, even if it were inferred from the history of the genres? But why should we refuse to attempt to outline a system of invariables which, fastidiously worked out, would perhaps help contemporary literature to get out of the disorder, confusion, and ugliness in which it so often dissipates, if not completely loses, itself? When poetry renounces rhyme, then rhythm, then speech, then the meaning of words, then punctuation, then words, to present itself under the form of isolated letters or groups of consonants which cannot be pronounced and are scattered at random on the page; and when the novel is sold in the form of a sheaf of papers which each reader can shuffle like a deck of cards, the comparative analysis of the structure of poems (whether the civilizations under study have or have not enjoyed historical relations) would permit us, perhaps, to discover the *sine qua non* qualities of the poem or novel *per se*. At a time when, either through derision or through defiance, so many people reject all aesthetic norms, or impose on themselves rules incompatible with the art they claim as their own, the comparative study of literatures, even of those which have not reacted one upon the other, would contribute to the restoration of contemporary art. Yes indeed, why should the comparatist always be passive? As for those who swear by Brecht and *distanciation*, why don't they demonstrate that *distanciation* existed long before that great man popularized the term? Why don't they try to revitalize the European or American theater by upholding the theory of the *Noh* through the performance of *Noh* plays? Was G. Woodberry so completely wrong when he wrote, in the first issue of the *Journal of Comparative Literature*, "the comparative method is the mother of all classicism"?

We must also recast our programs

However, we should recast our programs. The world in which the students we are now training will be teaching, the world for which they will have to prepare their own students, will probably have this composition: one or two billion Chinese who will claim to be of the first rank among the great powers; Moslems in hundreds of millions who, after having asserted their will to independence, will re-assert (as indeed they are already doing) their religious imperialism; an India where hundreds of millions will speak, some Tamil, others Hindi, still others Bengali, others Marathi, etc.; in Latin America tens of millions of Indians who will clamor for the right to become men again, and men with full rights; at least one hundred and twenty million Japanese, besides the two present great powers, Russia and the United States, who perhaps will have become allies in order to counterbalance new ambitions; a huge Brazil, a Latin America perhaps at long last rid of United States imperialism; a Black Africa exalting or disputing *négritude*, etc. As for us Frenchmen, we are quite willing to create an *Agrégation* of Modern Letters, provided, however, that it does not include China or the Arab world. Under the pretext that a strange audacity is needed "to foresee thus the intellectual preoccupations and the tastes of the faraway future," Adrien Cart, General Inspector of Public Instruction and President of the Examination Jury for the *Agrégation*, limits his objective to preparing young men who would do a fairish job of teaching around 1870. We will continue to talk of Ariosto, *Don Quixote*, the *Thousand and One Nights*, but the "subjects too far removed from the habitual preoccupations of Professors of French or Comparative Literature" he eliminates from our programs. It seems to me, on the contrary, that we have not chosen our profession to follow sheep-like "the habitual preoccupations" of uncultured and conformist minds. In the same way that the very nature of our discipline invites us to dream of a rhetoric powerful enough to act on literature in the making, our discipline also commands us to orient the minds of our students, not only in the direction of these questions which are being raised today, but also and more especially in the direction of those which will arise in the future.

... thinking of the year 2050 ...

Instead of teaching comparative literature in miserable Institutes where a single professor and his assistant can treat with competency no more than a very few subjects, it would be desirable, as I mentioned at the beginning, to centralize the teaching of comparative literature in order to be able to offer the students of comparative literature all kinds of subjects, a few samples of which follow:

The influence of French positivism in Latin America; Contacts between Jews, Christians, and Moslems in Andalusia; Western influences during the Meiji era; Role of the discovery of Japan on the formation of liberal ideas in the century of the Enlightenment; Evolution of racist ideas in Europe since the discovery of America and Black Africa; Evolution of the European novel in the 20th century under Russian and American influences; Effect of the American movie on French (or German, or British) literature in the 20th century; Comparative poetics of the *Noh* and of tragedy (or of the *kyogen* and the farce); Bilingualism in colonized countries; The influence of bilingualism on literatures; The diffusion of Taoism in Europe between the 18th and 20th centuries (or Zen, even); The influence of Russian (or French, or English) syntax on the evolution of the *paihoua*.

These are some of the hundred, the thousand subjects which a comparatist fully aware of today's world can suggest to his students and which could be treated in an Institute organized as I suggested. Each of the countries, needless to say, would center its teaching on a certain number of questions which especially interested it, and I can imagine that in France particular attention would be paid to the interactions of Western literatures, while in Russia and Eastern Europe comparatists would particularly concentrate on the singular situation of that part of the world. That in Russia comparative literature should be more especially concerned with Slavic studies and the relations between the different literatures of the peoples of the Union seems to me reasonable and fair. But I would wish that, in all countries where our discipline is taught, a truly international association of comparative literature would propose a certain number of subjects of general interest which would be treated *everywhere,* in order to show students of this planet that each literature owes something to all others, and precisely what they owe one another. This would favor the union of thinking minds.

. . . and our researches by organizing them . . .

A program of research elaborated also by comparatists from around the world, and which would attempt first of all to fill the gaps in our discipline, should direct us to create teams of researchers trained to treat those subjects about which knowledge is lacking. In a century when we have finally understood that we can no longer leave to caprice or chance either the subsistence of peoples or their economy I am surprised that we leave in a condition of perilous anarchy this portion, at least, of the life of the mind which can and indeed must organize itself. As much concerned as anyone else with freedom, I would not have the feeling I was being imposed upon if, in common agreement with my colleagues, I were appointed to teach more particularly that part of our discipline for which I might find myself possessing some competency and some feeling. I do not see in what way a colleague from another country could consider himself oppressed if a truly international organization, appreciating his talents and his knowledge, suggested that he devote himself to comparative metrics. Thus, gaps would be filled without fear of waste through the duplication of efforts, efforts which could be distributed all the more efficaciously since everything of importance to our discipline remains to be done, and so much the better for our successors.

IV

CONCLUSION

As I reread these pages, I wonder how I dare assemble and propose so many commonplaces. Is this the *enfant terrible* of comparative literature? Is that all there is? Commonplaces, yes indeed, but commonplaces which the "French school" long held to be radical and revolutionary. Since I am less impressed with the novelty of an idea or a doctrine than I am with its accuracy, it matters little to me if I find here and there, and even among the pioneers of our discipline, suggestions and even more of the ideas I hold today after nearly thirty years of teaching. Does not G. E. Woodberry's formula, "the comparative method is the mother of all classicism," which I mentioned previously, go back to 1903? If I am an *enfant terrible*, here are two others at least: René Wellek and Austin Warren who state, in their *Theory of Literature:* "The study of comparative literature in this sense will make high demands on the linguistic proficiency of our scholars. It asks for a widening of perspectives, a suppression of local and provincial sentiments not easy to achieve." If I am an *enfant terrible*, please direct the same compliment (or the same reproach) to A. L. Willoughby of London, who, in his criticism of English comparatism, uses the terms I have just used, or not far from it: "This point of view, however imperfect it might be, shows clearly that we, specialists in comparative literature, have not thus far, properly speaking, done much more than marginal studies, that we have concerned ourselves mostly with peripheral problems dealing for example with sources, themes, diffusion, the value or even the raw material of literature, or with some primarily sociological manifestations of its action. However valuable studies of this kind might be in order to make us aware of the spiritual exchanges in the course of the last centuries, they reveal to us at the same time to what extent our methods are limited."

As you can see, I am not alone in Europe in judging our methods and conceptions with harshness, neither am I the only one to plump for stylistics, or even rhetoric: "In the course of these last years, a very healthy reaction has set in a little everywhere in literary criticism, and we have again come to recognize that any study in literature must start with the text itself. The former methods of classical rhetoric, poetics, and metrics have been restored and renewed, while language and style, far more so than content, are at the heart of our research. And morphological considerations play an increasingly important role." Have I said anything other than this? And when I beg that we give to the translator what is due to him, and to translations our esteem, I am again simply confirming what Willoughby has said: "And now we are again brought back to the question of translation, so urgent for the comparative literature specialist." Yes, indeed, I wish all genres in all literatures to be studied, whether they have or have not *relations of fact*. Such is indeed the concern of Professor A. T. Hatto, of London, when he studies the aubade from China to Goethe by way of Shakespeare.

What appears to me encouraging, or conclusive, is that I have reached these ideas by myself and that, on the strength of a principle precisely fundamental to the oldest rhetoric, *"nullius addictus jurare in verba magistri,"*[18] I have chosen to read the theorists of our discipline only after elaborating some ideas springing from my indissociable experience as professor and writer.

[18] Horace, *Ep.* I, 1. 14.